GOD
AND THE
NEW HAVEN
RAILWAY

GOD
AND THE
NEW HAVEN
RAILWAY

AND WHY NEITHER ONE IS DOING VERY WELL

GEORGE DENNIS O'BRIEN

BEACON PRESS • BOSTON

Beacon Press
25 Beacon Street
Boston, Massachusetts 02108

Beacon Press books are published under the auspices
of the Unitarian Universalist Association
of Congregations in North America.

92 91 90 89 88 87 86   8 7 6 5 4 3 2 1

Library of Congress Cataloging in Publication Data
O'Brien, George Dennis, 1931–
   God and the New Haven Railway and why neither one is
doing very well
   1. God.   2. Religion.   I. Title.
BT102.028   1986   291   86-47554
ISBN 0-8070-1010-3

Text design by Christine Leonard Raquepaw

*Anguish is opposed to the spirit
of seriousness . . .*
Jean-Paul Sartre

Contents

Contents

God and
the New Haven Railway

A book has to have some title. This one came to me while trying to go back to sleep at three A.M. The subject matter of these writings is God or gods and/ or religions. In a secular age any book which announces itself straight off on those topics, however, is not likely to find an audience. More important, I fear that a book so grandly titled won't find its subject matter either. God, I hope, is as much put off by most books about Himself and religion as I am. There are, to be sure, magnificent theological efforts, and yet the most magnificent often turn out not to be about God straightway but Summas of almost everything one can sweep together, or diaries of seducers who take a strange turn and end up spiritually smitten. The Bible turns out to be about all sorts of things—including God.

If God may be put off by earnest efforts on his behalf, one supposes that a goodly number of readers are somewhere between bored and huffy at the prospect of a "God book." Gods, like penguins, may not be their thing; or gods, like dragons, may be regarded as remnants of antique and barbarous times now left well enough alone. This book argues that gods cannot be ignored since our understanding of the "merely human" is determined by how we fit ourselves into the mechanisms, organisms, and other devices (if any) of the universe. We have been very much exercised of late about the human attitude toward "the lower orders": snail darters, bald eagles, and beef cattle. Presumably there are equally interesting problems with "higher orders": androids, angels, and on up. There has been much cinematic speculation recently about higher beings courtesy of Darth Vader and his henchpersons. This book attempts to give the Bible equal time with Steven Spielberg. Even if the Bible were to turn out to be religious fiction on a par with *The Return of the Jedi*, raising the issue of human rank in the actual (or possible) order of things is no marginal matter. Unless one has already decided that humanity is cosmic top-of-the-line—and I would rather expound all of the *Summa Theologica* than try to make that case—then deciding where humanity falls in the order of perfections relative to actual Martians or speculative Gods (or vice versa) is a compelling task.

If humanity is to be located on some actual or imaginary scale of cosmic capacities, then we will have to survey the orders "up" and "down." I mean no moral slight to clams and other crustacea by putting them "down," but it does seem appropriate to scale various beings in terms of their range of interests and behaviors. Clams seem more settled than humans, and humans in turn have imagined gods and others even more adventuresome than themselves. The conventional top has been labeled "god." By assessing ourselves in terms of our betters (or the Best) we can decide what good humanity itself should be up to.

I assume we don't know very much about God—we may not even be sure that there is a subject for "the biography of God" (or perhaps it is not a person but a syndicate?). However vague we may be about "the divinity story," it seems plausible that any deity worth writing about will have a hard time managing the role. A proper divinity cannot arrive on the stage in quite the same fashion as Barbra Streisand. She is a character among characters dealing with types like Ronald Reagan and Omar Sharif. If one proposes to write into any scenario a deity character who is the All-in-All, one will find it difficult to keep him/her/them/it from becoming frightfully mixed up with all the other characters as well as the scenery and the props. It would be as if one started off to paint a portrait of Streisand but it kept looking like Gloria Steinem or the Statue of Liberty.

Which leads to the New Haven Railroad. If God is a ubiquitous character stealing all the scenes, playing all the roles in disguise, He can be found in or at almost anything: Barbra Streisand, Grant's Tomb, or the New York, New Haven, and Hartford Railroad. Why pick on the New Haven? Because neither God nor the railroad seems to be running very well these days. Worst than that! The New Haven's modern career bears a somber resemblance to our modern attitude toward deities. A long history of unreliability leads to nonexistence. Right or wrong, the average commuter seems to have given up on the New Haven and on God. Perhaps this book should be viewed as spiritual Amtrak—an attempt to keep religion running.

When I was in college some thirty years ago, the

railroad station in New Haven was a moderately grand affair. It boasted marble floors, elaborate brass clocks, airy ceilings, and pretentious entrances. It was a foyer for a heady trip to the big city and beyond. When I returned for a twenty-fifth reunion, I discovered that the station had been abandoned. All that remained of that elegant monument to travel was a shed attached to the original building. What struck me in the sleepless hour when I concocted the title for this book was that religion (if not Deus himself) seems to have suffered a similar fate. Where Church and Temple were once grandiose constructions suggesting all sorts of adventurous journeys to the beyond, they seem today reduced to humanity's arrivals and departures. (Since writing this paragraph, I have learned that the railroad station has been elegantly restored. I could wish a similar fate for the ecclesiastical enterprise.)

There is another reason for bringing God onto the New Haven. A book should have an audience—at least one large enough to justify waking up at three in the morning. What audience is there for these quasi-semi-theological reflections? I will settle for regular commuters and occasional shoppers. It is altogether fit and proper that sacred mysteries should be revealed to adolescent French farm girls, but it would be nice if someday the Lord—or one of his angelic assistants—were to epiphanize on the 5:17 to Larchmont. A God who travels only on camels may end as a subject only for tourists, not for life's daily commuters.

How is the modern commuter to engage his or her imagination with that Biblical narrative so overstocked with sheep and figs? This is no small problem. To the extent that the leading divine character proves elusive, he or she should be sensed in the texture of life. Can dacron be that texture? Sober heads have suggested that we abandon the sanforized fabric of modern technological society in order to rediscover God in the elementary woof of nature in which the Biblical narrative was founded. There is much to be said for the return to simple sources, but many of us are ill at ease confining an energetic deity to any corner of existence, be it mountaintop, monastery, or Manhattan.

If the deity appears in dacron, that also tells us *where* he may be spied out—and it is not by any means in churches and shrines as if the sacred were cooped in the tabernacle. If that were true, then deity would be an item somewhere on the shopping list of the week: dry cleaning, dairy products, deity. Church or Temple is not a place to locate some additional item for the week, it is a place from which one surveys the life list. Churches are vista points. From the mountaintop one does not see anything one would not see on the ground. What happens up there is that the whole is organized in a perspective that reveals patterns that can only be guessed at down here. Deity is already down there, in every nook and precinct with the churchgoers and the commuters equally, but we lack the perspective to see how this is so. We must also remember that what is real is the landscape; the vista point is not itself the object to be seen. A great deal of church life operates as if one went to the top of the Empire State Building to view the isle of Manhattan and the attendant insisted that one spend the time admiring the binoculars.

A sensible guide at some notable vista will, of

course, give us specific directions on where to look for the interesting objects. This is not easy in a god book. A theological writer wants to talk about everything, but the everything has to be organized in certain perspective. It is like a children's puzzle in which we try to find hidden faces drawn in the trees. The viewer *already* sees everything, all the lines are on the page, but he can't see the lines of the leaves *as* faces. A helping teacher has nothing more to reveal to the perplexed viewer. She does not say, "Look, under the flyleaf. See there is a face." Rather she says, "Here, try looking at it this way! Tilt it a bit! See that line and that!" This book offers suggestions on how to tilt things.

A sensible author should admit that the task of a deity book is distinctly odd. The author is not at all a proper teacher handing over facts and theories to an unknowing student. The master and the pupil have all the facts right there in broad daylight and all the teacher can suggest is that the other one stand on his head, squint, and lean to the side. A third person observing these gimmicks may surely think that nothing terribly serious is going on. I accept that view; therefore this is not a very solemn work. These essays are concocted on the ground of a certain unavoidable foolishness in the enterprise. If the tone is less than reverential it is not because the whole business isn't finally awestriking but because the revelation point can be so prosaic. "Who would have expected that getting a free picnic lunch of fish and sandwiches would have struck them so—and twelve baskets left over as well!"

This book is not a book of *proofs*. I am not sure that one can prove the existence of God or the truth of religions. The concern that prompted this effort is not that commuters no longer know or believe the faiths of their forebears but that they find these ancient creeds only bizarre. Today religion is viewed as a series of fairy tales with moral lessons attached. The Bible gets shelved with Dr. Seuss. My hope in these pages is to explain to the reader skeptical of tall tales why our pastoral ancestors felt compelled to talk about (and believe in) gods and holy lands—and I want to emphasize that the idea of *God* cannot be replaced in this tradition for some more comfortable idea: the moral law, human progress, or the GNP. The Biblical story may finally fail to capture reality, but if its story is not meaningful (and true), psychic consequences are striking and profound. Biblical religion may well be rejected, but that is not quite like deciding that Santa Claus is a childhood fiction. If this unserious little book can make that clear it will accomplish its purpose.

At the conclusion of this book there is a scholarly appendix which will direct the reader to more sober treatments of the subject. God, knowing all, may take himself seriously, but the theological writer works with lesser wisdom. A wary playfulness is better measured to the human author's capacity to prounounce on solemn subjects. Though I am interested in deities in general, the one I particularly have in mind is the one who keeps turning up in the Bible. I was tempted to decapitalize the divine—in the spirit of locating the sacred on the local—but finally resorted to convention since the Biblical deity is unique enough to be singled out as God. I would like to desexualize "God," but whatever God is, he/she is not a hyphenated expression. So I refer traditionally and pronomially to "Him." May She forgive me.

7

One-Way Ticket to Grand Central

Where is the sacred on the New Haven Railway? That is the problem of this book. Presumably He is to be found on the local because we have ruled out flashy deities who travel in limos or on camels. Is the Good News covered by *The Wall Street Journal?* Consider the commuter's life condition. The one thing you can count on from the New Haven is that it can't be counted on. Recently a power station blew out and trains crawled from New Rochelle for months. Such is the exisential predicament of the human ticketholder. This book argues that spying the sacred is having a view on how things work. On the New Haven things don't work too well.

A mathematical frustration index (FI) can be derived by taking the time of the commuter's first appointment (A) multiplied by the dollar value of the client ($C\$$) divided into the length of delay (t) after New Rochelle: $FI = t/(A \times C\$)$. The average commuter on an average day can experience up to 7.3 on a 10-point scale. Because casual shoppers have no fixed appointment (A), their Frustration

er, and an occasional Oriental tourist
own to achieve a value approximating
s is, of course, very scientific. The only
idex rating of zero is for the physics of
es—both railway cars and passengers.
of the trip is completely reliable, be-
ility" is what human desire adds to
:ess. If I have an accident (break my
no "accident" in physical or physiolo-
ature is always "in order." That is why
physics has a frustration index of zero. Our human
problems, power brownouts, derailments, and hot
boxes are all perfect expressions of the laws of physics.

Once one establishes an unreliability factor, the
field of the sacred lies open. All basic life strategies
deal with the unreliability of almost everything. The
Peter principle, Murphy's law, Parkinson's dilemmas, and a host of other deep theological excursions
have offered analyses of the ontological crises of
fundamental *Dasein*. (*Dasein* is the invention of the
philosopher Martin Heidegger. It means, in literal
translation, to be there, and Heidegger commentators assure me he meant being struck on a local,
south of 125th Street.) When things don't work,
when we are *da*, we get the fundamental revelation:
things don't always work out as we desire. This
omnipresent, insistent revelation is the basic consideration in discussion of gods and associated en-
terprises.

The Frustration Index described in Murphy's various laws, principles, and dilemmas measures the
discrepancy between human desire and physical or
social functioning. Human beings have developed
several grand strategies for removing the frustra-

tion factor. Religions are the grandest strategies—
and the most desperate.

One direct ploy to avoid frustration is to reduce
desire. The Japanese businessman tourist who finds
himself *da* below 125th Street may possess sufficient
Oriental wisdom to reduce his Frustration Index by
this strategy. If he is a Zen perfect master, he may
actually achieve pure zero—though it is highly unlikely that many perfect masters travel for Toyota.
The Oriental religious way of life has as its main
thread the view that *desire* is the friction in the equa-
tion. Desire is illusion. The Oriental tilt causes the
hectic world of desires to reveal itself as pure surface
illusion. All that hurrying uptown, midtown, and
downtown becomes a distant airy pageant when
viewed from on high.

What marks the Oriental game plan as insistently
religious is the claim by the grandest masters that *all*
desire is illusion. Religious people like univeral
claims. Most folks not working in advertising are
willing to admit that at least *some* desires are illusions. I really didn't need another magazine sub-
scription. Yoga masters are more ruthless. Even
so-called necessary desires are jettisoned, starting
with the more spectacular ones like sex and daily
eating. One moves toward real mastership as one
reduces the need to eat to absolute minimum, and
starving to death may be a prized step on the road to
perfection.

The Oriental strategy for the life-game is ancient
and powerful; the spiritual tradition is rich and subtle; defeat of desire for a commuter culture obsessed
by consumption can prove strikingly attractive. In
the hippier days of the sixties, young folk revolted
against the commuter/consumption culture of their

parents by beading out in the direction of Orientalism. The Beach Boys toured the college circuit doing a double bill with the Mahareshi Mahesh Yogi. It is no insult to the urges of the young to suggest that most of their Orientalism was far short of the stern widsom of the great teachers of the East: more like hi-fi Hinduism.

An alternative grand plan for reducing frustration to zero is reducing physical malfunction to zero. The Western response to life—marvelously oversimplified—can be seen as the precise reverse of the Oriental. Instead of readjusting inner psyche to reduce desire to naught, we readjust outer physics. This is the "religion of technology." Given any known coefficient of unreliability, the American response is likely to be "Fix it!" While sober individual reflection may be skeptical of the universal applications of the dictum, there is a sense in which the spirit of our culture affirms a universal, unflagging technology. If the stranded stockbroker thinks the Buddhist businessman a trifle daffy for trying to alleviate frustration by defeating desire, the Oriental is likely to think there is something distinctly zany about hoping to get a technological fix for everything.

The religious game plan has a genuine itch to solve *everything*. All desires can be set aside; all technical problems can be solved. Both statements have a grandiosity which discomforts common sense. Isn't the sane course to see the world as a mix of fixes and frustration? One who seeks sanity—rather than the sacred—will divide the world by thought and common sense into the fixable and the utterly busted.

The spiritual adequacy of commonsense options

is a critical issue for religion. If one can really make the division between fixed and forever down— more important if one can *live* with the distinction— then this will determine whether religion makes any sense or is best left to sore losers and lunatics. If only convinced Zen masters and Fortune 500 CEOs can believe in the utter defeat of desire or the total triumph of the tool, what about the spiritual proletariat?

Eminent sanity might conclude that life is a mix of the fixable and the insurmountable. There should be a cure for the common cold, but curing the New Haven or death may be problems that exceed human capacity. If one grasps the state of the world in that fashion, there are distinguished, dignified, practical, nonreligious attitudes which can be adopted. The classical Romans were sensible folk with small use for the religions of the wild east of the empire. They borrowed as their favorite philosophies two second-tier Greek theories: Stoicism and Epicureanism. (The Roman urge to practicality rendered the bolder speculations of Plato and Aristotle unsuitable.) It is no wonder then that pragmatic Americans seem to repeat the Roman taste in philosophers. Stoicism and Epicureanism offer sensible lifestyles for the work-a-day commuter. Stoicism says grin and bear it, brownouts and death are inevitable. Such events are unfortunate but they really don't count that much anyhow. The other school, the Epicureans, received bad press from the Christian Church fathers, but they were the original sages of suburbia. Epicurus was the founder of the metaphysics of gardening; if one tends one's acreage in Palo Alto and doth not strive for the big fix-it strategy, then one will not take the railroad to neurosis and a high rating on the Frustration Index. In essence both Stoics and Epicureans adopt similar life plans: set limits and live within them. Zen masters, J.P. Morgan, Francis of Assisi, and like-minded folk show a distinct streak of irrationality by pretending that one can push too far beyond the limits of the mess in which we find ourselves.

Stoicism and Epicureanism establish fundamental life strategies based on plausible sanity. Unfortunately, humans have shown an incurable craving for more extravagant life plans. At the heart of the Roman strategy is the notion that a sane man limits his bets. Stick to the garden, don't expect too much from life or the patent office. If you can't cultivate your garden (Epicurus), at least cultivate your soul (Stoics). (*Soul:* antique term recently outdistanced by such scientific notions as ego, self, and "number one.") A bit of judicious fence work that sets limits on what is to be cultivated in the back yard or the brain will prevent the inevitable frustration when things break down.

The search for limiting and simplifying is very much with us in all the spiritual fix-it books that populate the nonfiction best-seller list of the *New York Times.* From the grand strategies of ecologists who decry the insanity of extrapolating technologies to the simpler handbooks for homemade serenity, we are encouraged to limit, to accept limit, to stop asking ourselves impossible questions.

The mark of psychic rationality is that one rations emotional attitude to realistic possibility. Limited possibilities should be rationed to limited emotional attitude. The child who cries over the vanished soap bubble has placed too much emotional commitment on the eminently extinguishable. Stoicism and Epicureanism are life strategies which recommend that emotional attitude be properly rationed to a world of fixed limits—otherwise one finds one's emotional credit overextended and psychic bankruptcy is next in line. Religion is spiritual Chapter 11—in perpetuity. On first hearing, setting limits sounds splendidly sane, but how shall we set the proper limits on our commitments, contracts, and life wagers? Consider the great Stoic Epictetus:

> In everything which pleases . . . or supplies a want, or is loved remember to add . . . what is the nature of each thing . . . If you love an earthen vessel, say it is an earthen vessel . . . for when it is broken you will not be disturbed. If you are kissing your child or wife, say it is a human being you are kissing, for when the wife or child dies, you will not be disturbed.

This Stoic injunction is superbly rational. Friends and lovers are a bit more substantial than soap bubbles or earthen pots, but hardly trustworthy in perpetuity. A bit of sober planning for death or divorce right from the start will avoid unnecessary pain at the end. The mating habits of many stylish Americans appear to conform to Roman caution. "Contractual" arrangements have moved from boardroom to bedroom so that everyone may have the life consolation of a limited-risk partnership.

Determining limits (if any) is the basic issue for a life strategy. If you accept a strategy for rationing emotional attitudes, then a species of more or less acceptable humanism will emerge as your lifestyle: a plain serviceable wardrobe with no fantasy frills. The religious impulse, by contrast, is woefully discontented with the sobriety of the Epicureans and the Stoics. The proper rations for emotional commitments are a case in point. A clue that Christians reject the Stoic counsels of limitation is their persistent belief in immortality. Without getting into the stage setting of immortality (hunting, singing, and traipsing in the clouds), the notion of beyond-mortality is an example of trying to stretch reality to fit an overdrawn emotional bank account. If you choose a lover without a contract for limited risks, then you are accepting either an irrational emotion or a supperrational reality. Whether or not traditional religious marriages were made in heaven, it appears that the emotional attitude entailed required that they be *finished* in heaven.

Let's begin with the assumption that religion starts at the point where human beings find themselves stuck with an emotional attitude that won't fit commonsense reality. Religion is a form of life overcommitment. A skeptical view of the religious urge suggests that one trim back a bit. Those who recognize the fragility of even the best, the sexiest, the sturdiest of friends and lovers preset their emotional attitudes so that loss can be taken with some measure of serenity. "That's life. What did you expect?" says common wisdom shuffling away from the inevitable flop. How strange that human beings reject simple common wisdom and keep entangling themselves in vast overcommitments to lovers and causes, corporations and communes.

Any sane view of the world—even the religious—will determine that there are some limits to be accepted, some desires that are phony and worthy of frustration. F. H. Bradley, the English philospher, rejected the notion of immortal life because so many people seemed to desire this state only so they could be reunited with their beagles. If religion finds solid spiritual ground, it will be because it addresses worthy desires impossible to abandon. The desire that drives true religion should be so central to the dignity of humanity that jettisoning God is tantamount to abandoning the central theme of the human story.

Religion arises, then, from frustration. Some desire overruns its capacity for realization, and humanity is forced to strike an attitude toward the limit revealed. One can decide that the specific desire is phony and the attendant frustration only the illusion of false temptation. Such retail assessments of desires are the stuff of common sense. Religion takes off when one is no longer able to bargain away desires. A real, unavoidable, and deeply moral desire collides with a seemingly insurmountable barrier. This collision establishes the starting point for the distinctly religious. Eastern religion tends to solve the dilemmas of desire by declaring *all* desires illusory. Biblical religion takes a different course. While some garden-variety desires are declared off-limits, there is a deep core of human longing that cannot be dismissed and yet cannot be realized—at least by human wit and will. In this tradition one needs help from the top to solve the frustration of the human heart.

The next two chapters examine the logic of frustration. While the quota of quandaries for humanity overflows, there is a simple structure to the array of anxieties we face. Are the checks on our desires many and disconnected or is there some single system underneath it all? Are the checks on human aspiration just part of the natural territory or have they been put there because someone is after us? If these are the issues, the religious terrain can be divided along quite traditional lines: polytheism versus monotheism (many troubles or one insistent trouble); impersonal versus personal ("natural" or "god"). Religious and nonreligious views are established by assessing whether our troubles are connected or haphazard, the ultimate actions of a willful God or natural outcomes.

Mafia and Godfather

Religion arises in railroad delays and other more aggravated frustrations. The limits on our longings need to be conned with a careful eye, of course. In the past, human folk were even more hemmed in than in the latter years of the twentieth century. A cure for acne has been announced. A manic optimist may come to think that everything is curable and that finally all barriers will fall. I assume that no such optimists ride the rails these days. When faced with the inevitability of being crimped in and lorded over by implacable powers, human beings have a fascinating repertoire of behaviors. Religions are part of that repertoire. We don't always take striking attitudes toward great limitations—a happy mind keeps busy with the garden as Epicurus commends—but in the end, at the end we are forced to say something even if it is *sic biscuitus disintegrat.* And there are many ways of crumbling life's little desserts.

Religious questions are always raised at frontiers, borders, limits, horizons. Anyone trafficking at social or metaphysical border checkpoints is negotiating in basic religious stuff. Whether one joins the Methodists, chants mantras, or merely mutters depends on what one decides about the meaning of these borders. Are they invitations to an "other side" or realistic cautions to stay home.

If religion starts from frustration, we would like to know whether the apparent borders of human aspiration are under anyone else's control and, if so, is there a means of getting a valid passport. We may decide that the frontiers are natural checks—metaphysical Himalayas that no human could scale and where no spiritual, superior sherpa could assist. Humanity is set in a borderland of implacable, insurmountable, and impersonal limits. There might be some super ones who could offer a helping hand. Not all superiors are interested in helping out, however. The Stoics believed that there were gods but that these "immortals" were having such a good time being wise that they had no interest in human prayers and petitions. On the other hand, one might believe that there were immortals interested in dabbling in human affairs but that they hadn't come up with a sensible game plan. It is this classical Greek view, polytheism, that I want to examine before turning to the more coherent monotheisms of Mother Nature or Father God.

A universal American complaint is "What have *they* done now?" "They" seems to be everywhere up to dirty tricks on our innocent citizenry. Sometimes "they" is an ill-starred ethnic group or other identifiable entity, but often it is merely a fuzzy collective of dimly perceived hostile forces: City Hall, Wall Street, the Sanitation Union. The belief that our personal world is surrounded by scarcely benevolent gangs ready to rain out the office picnic is breathtakingly realistic. Ancient polytheism projected a celestial Mafia related to the human populace by a loose connection of extortion and bribery. Security was minimal because there was a perpetual gang war on Mt. Olympus so that a payoff to Posiedon might get you shot up by Zeus. The Trojan War, as Homer sets it down, shows a neighborhood caught in the middle of an internal feud of the heavenly heavies. It was tough on the humans who were largely stand-ins for the various Olympian dons.

Polytheism has been scorned by the dominant monotheistic religions of the West, but as a description of life as we live it, one has to say that it appears eminently sensible. Polytheism starts with a plausible platform. It claims that human folk are surrounded by superforces both capable of and willing to lord it over us and that these superforces haven't got their act together. From the standpoint of my personal week's agenda, life seems the zany outproduct of a highly antagonistic set of partly benevolent, mostly bored, occasionally nasty overlords. They are making a mess of my life! Surely the epic of my life is being produced, directed, and distributed by a studio in a major managerial crisis—they can't even decide whether it is to be a comedy or a tragedy or whether my part is to be played by Clint Eastwood or Porky Pig. My lines are inconclusive, I missed my big scene, and they are writing in my exit at the wrong time—it is always the wrong time to exit.

Sophisticates may snicker at personalizing the superforces, but the basic inspiration is sound. The ancient Romans, for instance, had a goddess of fever. Of course the fever was caused not by the goddess but by mosquitoes in the undrained marshes. On the other hand, mosquitoes might qualify in a sophisticated polytheism as superforces quite beyond human control. Any sane view of the human situation would define our life as surrounded by forces beyond human control ranging from earthquakes to sex, death, and mosquitoes. It also seems sensible on a first pass to say that these various life-lords are in a state of perpetual feud. Earthquakes, mosquitoes, and death can all interfere seriously with one's sex life. And if Freud is right, sex interferes with absolutely everything.

Mosquitoes and sex are *natural* obstacles to human happiness and so we turn to that subject in the next chapter. But before abandoning polytheism, I want to emphasize how compelling the polytheistic scenario is to the average newspaper reader. It is no exaggeration to say that (nature aside) social polytheism is the great American religion. An anthropologist from the twenty-fifth century, having studied reruns of prime-time news, would surely come to such a conclusion. American life as there reported reads like *Polytheism II*, a script dominated by gods, demigods, and superheroes. Herbert Gans in *Deciding What's News* concluded that for CBS, NBC, *Time*, and *Newsweek*, news is what happens to approximately one hundred great persons in America and around the world. The top person is the president of the United States, and anything that happens to him is news. Thus, when the president does nothing—takes a vacation—it gets attention. A big story is when two great persons meet—the interest is not in what they do, it is in the meeting of greats. The result of "news-is-great-persons" is a fascinating recasting of social life on the polytheistic model. It isn't whether the president or the senator is correct on a matter of policy—you can seldom discover what the policy question is at all—it is whether the quarrel has "strained relations" between Great #1 and Great #2. Who knows what the issues were that placed the gods on opposite sides between the Trojans and the Greeks? Who cares! The point was that it was a super-scenario with lots of jealousy, loyalty, bloodshed, and speechmaking. Great stuff for the *Iliad* and *People* magazine.

To the extent that the Great Persons can fundamentally alter our lives—by raising the prime rate or endorsing hula hoops—we live in a social framework of pragmatic polytheism. There are greater powers than I, so it pays to deal with these great ones for my own good. The whole commercial repertory of ancient polytheism from bribery to flattery will be brought to bear as a means of getting on the good side of the stars and newsmakers.

Polytheisms, however, are inherently unstable. Perhaps it is our limited intellect, but we do seem to insist on tidying up our spiritual world. At least it gives a nice ordered focus to one's paranoia instead of the dispersed anxieties of an ordinary week. Thus, just as nature polytheisms give over to an orderly Mother Nature, social polytheisms have a tendency to be replaced with social "monotheisms." And one again faces the same set of choices about personal versus impersonal. In social monotheism there is one Lord, one Don, one Godfather who is behind *everything*. Sometimes the one Lord is "impersonal" or collective: the government, the military-industrial complex, the Communists and their fellow travelers, the capitalists and their running dogs. Nor does one have to regard such unifying hypotheses as aimed only at villians; sometimes history is seen as in the hands of savings forces: the proletariat, the Northern Baptists, the Southern Baptists, the Hard Shell Baptists, etc. Impersonal monotheisms in human affairs have generally proved unsatisfactory and are usually replaced by "cults of personality." The rise of such cults of personality in Communist countries has a certain inevitability since communism offers a "monotheistic" theory of history in which the secret working of the proletariat class is all-pervasive and all-powerful. Such a scenario for dominance of *human* affairs suggests a human face in the forefront. To be dominated by a faceless proletariat may seem no better than being dominated by mosquitoes. Thus, despite a collectivist ideology, Communist regimes seem inevitably to sum up the movement in the figure of the noble helmsman whose every thought becomes a full expression of the commune—Mao as ultimate Godfather.

Insofar as our social gods are powerful agents with whom we might dicker and bargain, "religion" remains a business relationship with the normal range of risks and rewards. There is, however, a deeper religious urge at work in *Modern Screen*. It is unlikely that average readers of that magazine would describe their relation to great persons as an instance of infralapsarian substitutionary theology—yet the behavior of masses of people at the death of great and little heroes and heroines from John Kennedy to Janis Joplin suggest that precise characterization. It is not only that we want the great world to be dominated by personalities, not impersonal issues and causes, it seems that we would live and die in the lives of these persons. St. Paul says, "Not I, but Christ in me," and the rock fans says, "Not I, but Elvis, the King, in me." As one assesses a drab life hustling chips in Merseyside, it becomes much more interesting to live in and through the glory of John, Paul, Ringo, and George. The emptiness of my emotional life is filled with the triumphs and tragedies of the stars. This is infralapsarian substitutionary theology: in this time of emptiness and sin (lapse), I substitute the life of the gods (stars) for my own. My life is emptied out in the fullness of the jet set.

One may pity the rock-and-roll polytheist and the votaries of the Super Bowl, but one cannot deny the popularity of their commitment. At whatever level, polytheism rests in two strikingly persuasive notions: One, there are forces that lord over my life. Two, these forces are in conflict. Polytheism tends to score high on the Frustration Index. It is hard enough to be lorded over by superior powers and persons; it is even worse if these superiors squabble all the time. It has therefore been consoling for humanity to seek some rational order in the mishmash of conflicting forces. We look for an underlying unity in the multiple assaults on ordered existence. The unification of a polytheistic world can move in only two directions: an impersonal unity or a personal unity. Basic "religious" views stem from the type of unity chosen. A general "impersonal" unification rationalizes the greater forces into the notion of Nature. The alternative is a monotheism: the one God who supersedes the chaotic Olympian village. So it has been in Western culture. Although polytheism continues to live a vibrant life in pop culture, the high religions of the West have been natural science and Jewish monotheism. We turn now from Godfather Zeus and his polytheistic clan to the splendid unity of Mother Nature.

Jehovah Meets
Smokey the Bear

Any sensible view of the world holds to a basic, minimalist description that human life is hemmed in by events over which we have little control—like the tuition at Princeton. A rock-bottom view of life seems to suggest some sort of gods, lords, heroes, or bill collectors who are mastering desired parts of my domain. The spiritual choices available to the species are dictated by what we come to believe about these outside powers and how we decide to act, think, or feel about them. Only a technology freak is likely to deny the existence of superpowers; what has changed since the days of easy theism is the view that these superpowers are personal things that can be invoked and berated. You may do that to the university but not to the universe.

This book is interested in the Biblical view of superpowers. To make any sense out of the biblical divine, however, one has to start with deities as a class. I assume that from our point of view there are "superpowers"—humankind is not the cosmic controller. This chapter concentrates on a traditional superstar who has recently staged a terrific come-back: Mother Nature. By examining her traits and talents we can discover how she compares with and departs from the deity who prods the patriarchs of the Bible.

Nature admiration appears in many contemporary forms from the ecology movement to organic-food addiction. It is difficult to find a single core to the whole range of advocates who appeal to Nature as a guide to sanity and morality. Nevertheless, there is some rough thing slouching toward a common idea, and it can be seen most clearly in what is denied. A continuing theme in the Nature movement is the denial of the worship of technology. In this it makes a protoreligious move. If all there was to religion was the acknowledgment of powers superior to humans in the cosmos, then the Nature movement is a sure-fire religion. It has a goddess that only the U.S. Corps of Engineers would wish to deny.

The religious value of Mother Nature will be determined by the appropriate attitude we should take to such a *grande dame.* Sanity is measured by deciding whether an emotional attitude is appropriate to its object. To rage maniacally at weasels is decidedly bizarre. What is a sane attitude toward Nature? We have no problem deciding that certain attitudes are absurd. The technologist is absurd if he believes that Nature is a passive servant. Sanity suggests that Nature is an awesome force to ride with, not something to dream of diking overall.

Awe is a proper attitude before the might of the storm or the delicacy of the nerves—and awe is an emotion somewhere in the religious realm. The nature movement is more than a prudential caution to preserve enough oxygen, it is also concerned with maintaining awe in the city dweller's harried head. Nature lovers want to save the majestic crag so that humans may be better able to measure themselves. It would be impossible to have any religious sense without a sense of awe. Awe is an attitude held toward higher, cleverer, more powerful forces than are normally questioned by the Gallup Poll. It is a form of foolishness not to hold greater powers in awe, and it is a form of major unreality not to think that there are some such "powers" lodged in our environment. The nature of Nature religion depends on how humans come to terms with the Awesome.

By preaching a gospel of awe, the Nature movement makes a distinct contribution to our religious sense of life. At a minimum, Nature humbles man/woman in his/her pride and lifts up his/her eyes to the mountains. The problem for a Nature movement is not the first step but the second. Can Mother Nature, Blessed Be She, the Awesome One, offer a full religious prospectus for humankind? Salvation anywhere you can get it these days is not to be sneezed at, but if a Nature movement really competes with older religious traditions, we need further details about the Awesome One.

A point of essential difference between old-time religion and Nature religion is seen in the role of worship. Whether it is the Holy Bear or the Sacred Lamb, the object of the cult practice is to be worshipped. Worship is an attitude which depends on the Awesome; in life's great dry-goods sale, it is no good to worship seconds. Is the Awsome One also a Worshipful One? The Worshipful One must be awesome, but to be worthy of worship he, she, or it should have some characteristics over and above the ability to blow us off the beach. To be worshipped, the Awesome One must be regarded as recognizing—even in the midst of all its other business of tinkering with the galaxies and watching the cattle on every high hill—some dignity in human persons. Lacking such a peculiar interest, the Awesome One may get my contribution during the collection—a pay-off to heavenly powers—but not my worship. I leave before the communion service.

It takes a *grand jeté* of faith to vest Mother Nature with much maternal solicitude. Only yesterday, the Darwinian theory of evolution seemed to reveal "nature red in tooth and claw." "Survival of the fittest" was the propaganda slogan for evolution. Social Darwinists opined that peace propaganda was sentimental twaddle which was degenerating the gene pool of the human race. One imagines defendants at Nuremberg insisting that they were just part of a "back to nature" movement. A glance at Darwin's quarrelsome species and those philosophers of evolution should check the simple notion that Nature has all the winning ways of Smokey the Bear. There is a clear admonition in the Nature movement that if the technocrats don't exercise caution, Mother Nature will follow her certain chemical laws and our local pond will become a celestial cesspool. It is Nature's awesome *indifference* to human fiddling around that allows us to predict ecological apocalypse. In the New Testament apocalypse, Father God is *mad* at us.

A first pass at Mother Nature would suggest that awe is in order, worship is not. We reach again one of those basic decision points where the spiritual paths of various religions and their pious cousins

29

diverge. Common sense suggests that all human activity is encased in an environment of superpowers that we would be foolhardy to ignore. *Nature* is an omnibus term for a whole syndicate of superpowers. "Behold the Awesome, repent thy plastic ways!" Recognizing the Awesome is a step in the direction of any religious sense of life, but if the Awesome is Mother Nature, humanity may be (properly) humbled but not, as in Biblical religion, exalted (surprisingly).

Given dwindling attendance in churches and the soaring attendance at the National Parks, some earnest clerics may come to prefer Audubon over St. Paul. That can't be correct. Awesome, austere, and even rational as Nature religion may be, it is certainly *not* Biblical religion, and that should be obvious from almost any page of the text—O.T. or N.T. For better, and surely for worse, as far as the Nature sage is concerned, the Bible is full of precisley those little human intrigues that a sublime view of nature finds so dispiriting. There is Jacob cheating Esau, David itching for Bathsheba, apostles quarreling about preferment, Peter denying, and a whole supporting cast of warmongers, murderers, cheats, tax gatherers, hypocrites, and thieves (some of whom, admittedly, see salvation just in time). This record of faithlessness, apostasy, repentance, disaster, regeneration, and talk, talk, talk is supposed to be the deep spiritual message? It makes the Redwoods seem particularly inviting.

Some ecological strategists have noted correctly that the Bible is not a treatise on Nature worship and have even assigned it a villain's role in the story of environmental exploitation. There is considerable truth in the charge. Biblical religion starts with

Adam and Eve losing their lifetime pass to the park system. Nature and humanity have a falling out in the first few pages of *Genesis* that never gets patched up. Sheepherding and fig tending are not high-tech industries, but they are human activities accompanied by much clipping and dipping. It is by labor and tears that the children of Israel must win a living from an unfriendly Nature.

After that bad experience with the apple tree and all those years in captivity pushing stone blocks up an inclined plane, things don't improve much nature-wise after the Hebrews head out of Egypt. First of all they have forty years in the desert—not the most friendly side of Mother Nature's personality—where they must be sustained by miraculous springs of water and heavenly manna. They do make it to the promised land, flowing with milk and honey, but only over the memory of war and destruction. The rest of the Hebrew Bible is an uncheerful tale of civil war, external attack, captivity, and finally Roman imperial conquest. The nation survives on wit, faith, and the ability to manage long trips on short notice.

When the Hebrews find a God, then, He is measured to their persistent life experience. That persistent experience is not "cozied-in-with-nature." The consistent role for the Hebrew people runs along one line: exiles, nomads, captives, refugees, invaders, displaced persons, colonized, dispersed. Other folks might build temples for their gods; it is no surprise that Jehovah has to settle for a tent. Travel becomes a dominant Jewish metaphor for life.

If religion starts with a recognition of limits, then Mother Nature is a great setter of boundaries. There is nothing at all fanciful in regarding Nature as a superpower who holds us in her unfailing grasp. Nature "religion" is, therefore, a sober reaction of humankind to its territory. No fairy tales here—the fairy tale is the technologist-wizard story of mastering Nature by magic and transistors. However, if Nature is *the* superpower it is, we assume, an impersonal conglomerate awesome in might and main but sublimely indifferent to our small technologies and dynastic squabbles. It is that sublime indifference that a nature religionist would have us regard as the proper corrective to human pride. Biblical religion differs from nature religion in two extraordinary respects. First, it puts a much higher value on human dealings than Nature could possibly accept; second, and related, it has a superpower who can be addressed. Nature religion calls for austere silence; Biblical religion is mostly talk.

In Exodus the Jews fly out of Egypt into the desert where instead of discovering the great austerity of that overwhelming nature, they discover a God who talks. The desert is in itself a spiritual place of awesome silence; Moses turns it into an argument. In just that place where a sober Stoic, a sane scientist, or a sensitive Sierra Clubber finds the tranquility of everlasting quiet, the Jews take up an elaborate legal contract with Yahweh full of subcontracts, codicils, understandings, conditions, subparagraphs, and a dash of medical advice. Biblical scholars tell us that the Law stems from a later historical period, but the editor who anachronized the text had the right idea. This Hebrew God reveals himself when and where Nature is barren—not in trees and beasts but in the ever-present human coin of talk.

I am not interested here in whether all that negotiating actually took place on Mt. Sinai and other touristic sights of the ancient Middle East; I am only concerned to point out that the Hebrew deity, if He exists at all, is not Mother Nature. To be a decent divinity at all, one must of course be awesome. That is surely claimed from Genesis through the surrealist scenario of the Apocalypse at the conclusion of the Christian writings. But in addition to being awesome, this divinity parlays and protects.

Religion is not a matter of recognizing some super facts about our celestial neighborhood. Superpowers there are! Some of them are fair to awesome, and when they are swept together in a cover notion like Nature or Universe or the Great Process of Atoms, *very, very* awesome. Only the fool could say in his heart, that there is no Awesome One. The question is where our small dignity with its attendant possibility for minor vice and banal atrocity sits with the Awesome One. As for Mother Nature, it seems fair enough to say that she/it cares not at all for all that tawdry history of small achievement and scattered squalor which constitutes the planet's audited account. It is this which the Nature worshipper calls to our sober attention. The priestess of river, tree, and plumed hawk invites us to purge our consciousness of petty projects and merge with the sure, unfailing ever-moving loom of nature. Listen to the slow rhythm of the wave, the cries of faraway eagles, the soft lift of wind upon the endless desert sands.

Nature's stark beauty beckons us from the clamor of city and history into the eternal cycle of life and the seasons of our years. The vision is so compelling and so attractive that one can only wonder that Jews, then Christians, then Western civilizations have turned so steadfastly against it. In the East, Buddha, the Hindu sages, and philosphers of the Tao all look for rectifying human life by finding the great cyclic current beneath the scurrying ships of trade. Even Islam—though deeply connected to the Hebrew tradition, itself a religion of book and command—retains a strain of desert austerity more akin to worship of the Awesome One than the Holy One of the Hebrews. There is something peculiar—or perverse—about the Biblical divinity when compared to other awesome claimants for attention on the world horizon.

The Biblical divinity recognizes a peculiar value in the special human world that the Awesome divinity of the mountain and the storm cannot. If there is a peculiar *human* dignity, a peculiar worth to these hairless bipeds over and above their place in the wonderful silent sliding of the atoms, then the Awesome One of the Hebrew Bible is at least willing to recognize it. Jehovah reveals himself in and through a promise, a Covenant, and one does not *promise* except with another to whom one has granted extensive dignity. Promising always implies "And you might also refuse the offer. You are free to do so!" Imagine Mother Nature suggesting to any of her charges that they were free to turn down one of her propositions. Truly Mother Nature makes offers you can't refuse.

5

How to Be
a Really Superior Being

Social and natural monotheisms can be evaluated in
terms of their recognition of human worth. The
problem of being a really superior *theos* and taking
mannerly notice of these short featherless mammals
is considerable. One is tempted to think that a real
superior would consider them beneath notice, if not
contempt. This chapter examines the problem of
being both superior *and* religiously interesting.

When dealing with Superior Ones, one should
begin with a word about the freedom of us inferior
ones. Since freedom is where I would build a serviceable niche for human dignity, something
should be said about whether human freedom is a
reality. This book cannot examine in detail the
ancient conundrums about free will and determinism. Let me note, therefore, that there are those
who argue that freedom is an illusion. The radical
case is based on natural determinism and claims
that if we were sharp enough at the microscope, we
would see that our quadrennial presidential political campaigns are merely a muddling around of

molecules: Human behavior can be explained by lower-order natural events. The modest case claims only social determinism and alleges that the previously mentioned world historical events can be totally explained and predicted by a close study of somebody's real estate records: Human behavior can be accounted for by social occurrences in which the supposed actors played no role at all. In either natural or social determinst views, the action of the individual humans can be fully accounted for without taking the person's "acting" into account. Hiccupping is seldom a chosen action. Determinisms suggest that declaring war or promising marriage may be a similar involuntary spasm.

Such grand theories of determinism suffer from two fatal flaws. In the first place, no one seems to believe in them. Despite the acuity of the arguments offered, human beings continue to wander about praising and blaming one another for deeds done when, by rights, they should be huzzahing hydrocarbons and the Post Office—the true determiners of human action. In the second place, it is hard to think that pro-determinist authors believe their own theories since most such treatises are accompanied by earnest pleas to the reader to alter behavior in the light of the sober doctrine set down. But if I am as preprogrammed as the thesis suggests, it is difficult to see how I can be free to accept the suggestion. Most of us stick with the common sense— and wholly sensible—belief that human beings are free and responsbile actors. It is this ability to take free and responsible action that is the base for human dignity.

Anyone who stumbles across human freedom will soon discover, however, that it doesn't seem as extensive in action as it does in propaganda. We may be free, all right, but there are lots of things that humans can't seem to do at all: tie a bow tie, reform the Chicago City Council, or live forever. Our fundamental life strategy will be determined by deciding which of these areas of restriction are worth tackling *and* what to say or do (maybe nothing) about the really insurmountable. Religion—particularly Western religion (both classical and Biblical) in this case—seems to suggest that a well-documented *entente cordiale* with superior powers in the heavenly neighborhood would permit humanity to overcome some of the more oppressive of its apparent disabilities.

One of the most fundamental things we would like to know about dickering with superiors is whether it is worth the paperwork. One suspects that sending letters to Mother Nature about some of her engineering feats won't even get you a preprinted postcard in reply. Religions generally believe that there is Somebody you can write to. He, she, or they may be a bit slow on the turnaround but at least you won't waste a stamp. Obviously these cosmic bureaucrats must be folks of some authority since they control gates and crossings that we can't manage. It is because of these superior qualities that human beings have admired, adulated, adored, venerated, and even worshipped frontier controllers, "Gods and Heroes" we say. In our search for a deity, I want to consider what these elevated others would have to be like to get the top accolade.

One of the puzzles not attended to by science fiction writers is what constitutes a truly superior being. In science fiction we are constantly being confronted by saucers full of superior beings. The proof of their superiority is that they have invented laser razors and gravity warp thrust space commuter transport. They display superman-like physical powers: leap tall buildings, enjoy impenetrable skin and X-ray vision, and put up storm windows without getting a backache. Often these superior persons are evil—downright bad. They scheme and plot and connive like small-time hoods. Clearly we do not think that they are "superior" because of this moral fault, and most of the plot turns on how some low mortal defeats the superior brain and brawn of the space invaders.

A more interesting case would occur if the superior types did not display the usual range of human lusts but were in some sense morally indifferent to us or even morally superior. Suppose that the Martians, because they think so fast, are just downright bored with the slow-witted humans. Suppose they have some instant thought communication and won't bother to fathom this drawn-out noisemaking which we call talk. Suppose, in short, that being as ugly and slow as we are to their sophisticated minds and sleek bodies, they come to regard humans as chattel beasts. Not to be abused, mind you. One looks after cows for their usefulness. There is nothing downright wicked in this conduct, and in fact the Martians rather tidy up the planet. Would we regard these folks as superior? I think that we would not. Leave it at mere spiritual pride, but humans want to insist that they are not reducible to cash value even in a Martian cattle auction. We may be gauche and slow of thought, but we think that there is some intrinsic value, some basic freedom that human beings possess in fee simple that prevents any chattelizing of the species by any powers no matter how bright and beautiful.

Consider then the possibility of "morally superior" space creatures. These folks may decide to just wipe out the human race in justified moral indignation and disgust. Scurvy lot with their sweaty palms, dirty deals, Barbie dolls, and bayonets! One imagines them sweeping in from Mars like galactic Gary Coopers to clean up the frontier. Who could blame them—one would hardly recommend offering any history text as a brief for the defense. Yet it is clear enough that we would not finally regard the Martian marshalls as *really* morally superior—really superior at all.

The existence of superior beings in the universe is not at all hard to imagine. In fact, Carl Sagan, the TV impressario of the cosmos, considers it a relic of narrow religious persuasion that anyone would doubt their existence. The universe being so spaced out and ancient, there should be evolutionary processes going on all over the galaxies, and surely even Nature could do a better job out there than she had done locally. It could be taken then to be *highly* plausible that superior beings exist out there: brighter, stronger, and much prettier. It is also quite conceivable that they could have moral attitudes toward humans—if they ever sail in some day— ranging from common earthly venality to righteous indignation. In the long run the human judgment about superiority will rest ultimately on the outlanders' "moral" attitudes. Mere superior powers even in "persons" would be religiously empty if the super has not "proper" moral concern for me, and I should be quite prepared to return the courtesy.

Nor would I be impressed if the space master came up with little rewards if I acted appropriately. I wouldn't be impressed even if it was a *big* reward like a cure for cancer or a cure for funerals. If the Boss does these little favors just to show off or for amusement during celestial picnics, it would be a nice deal but I finally wouldn't give any moral credits.

Humans are (or ought to be) very choosy about what is worthy of religious approbation. If worship of a superior whats-it makes any sense at all, at least two conditions have to obtain: the object addressed has to be appropriately superior, and he/she/them must have certain attitudes toward the humans making all these approving noises. It makes no ethical sense to worship just any old thing. It is true that people have worshipped tree stumps and lizards, but they were always regarded as very special items of the kind. The lizard is the source of some overwhelming power that is evoked; it is the father of all stumps rooted in the primal earth. To worship at all is to accept that the object called upon is superior. Of course one can be factually wrong about the object. "Not that tree stump, you dummy, it is the one on the left!" But it is a piece of incoherence to say, "I worship her but she is thoroughly second rate." Having accepted that the thing worshipped or the power invoked is "superior" in some important and obvious sense, it is then necessary to realize that the superior must display a due regard for human dignity. Human dignity may not rank so high in the final cosmic audit, but it cannot be reduced to a write-off on a bad investment. That is a stringent condition for the superior one to meet, but it seems clear enough to our moral intuitions that a big-shot being out there who could do untold celestial tricks would not be worth a votive candle unless he/she had a "proper recognition" of the value of human existence.

The religious question is not as is so often supposed: Is there/are there any superpower(s) out there? The problem of religion is what is the proper human gesture toward the superpowers? Who are these superpowers, what are they like, and what should we think and feel in the face of the superpowers?

If we think that there are superior powers—and it seems only simple rationality that there are—we will certainly have attitudes toward them but only some of these attitudes would count as religious. In turn, religions themselves will differ on the nature of the Superior One and will strike differing sets of religious attitudes. We could believe that the superior powers are dumb—either silent or stupid. If they are powerful, underinformed bunglers, wariness would be a suggested attitude. An ordered, radically silent superior (great Nature herself) may elicit wonder but no commercial dealings or worshipful identification. Or there could be superior powers that are morally exemplary but simply have no regard for the human scene—like the rationalized immortals of the Stoics. Such types may be admired like some cosmic masterpiece, but one would not communicate with them any more than with the collected works in the Victoria and Albert Museum. Mighty works, full of moral inspiration, but they exist to be viewed, not invoked.

A further set of observations can be made about various religious superior beings. The God of Islam is a righteous power over and against the present world of flesh and blood. Salvation is surrender to the Almighty. Hindu deities in their multiple incarnations are friendly (sometimes antagonistic) powers who are closer to everyday life than the austere God of Mohammed. The peculiarity of the Jews in the Biblical story is not that they believe in superbeings while the idolatrous Jebusites and that lot do not. All these folks had gods and lesser allies under every bay tree and on every high hill. The Biblical religious problem is strictly What are we to say about the "gods" and how shall we act toward them? The interesting thing about the Hebrews is how they choose to talk to and about their god. It is more than mere accident that Judaism is a religion of the Book—it is this gesture of deciding to forge on in poems, prophecies, laws, pious stories, and ferocious preachments that characterizes a fundamental decision point for religious consciousness.

Perhaps a proper characterization of Biblical religious consciousness would note that these people insist on talking when any rational person would shut up. This incessant chatter makes sense only if there is "someone" to listen to all these murmurings who is not only not deaf but interested in the drift of the argument. The superior power we are looking for—if he is there and on duty—must be not only muscular but also a good listener.

6

Standing on Your Dignity While Riding Off into the Sunset

Freedom is one of the century's bright words. Everyone wants it and claims it: free markets, free love, free green stamps. Despite the wise necessitarians who would convince us to flow with Nature or accept our social lot as a mere pebble on the path of progress, there remains an insistent lobby for freedom that resists the course of acquiescence.

Freedom for the species is not just one of those nifty characteristics like naturally wavy hair; it is regarded as essential to our noncash value. Humans have been defined in lots of interesting ways from being featherless to being rational, but the interesting peculiarity of the species is freedom. This mode of differentiation is not part of a biological story—featherless will do for that—it is the basis of our "moral" story. It is the moral claim for essential freedom that leads to the belief that human beings must be *regarded* in certain ways. Thus we do not think it an appropriate attitude to take toward other humans that they be thought of as chattel beasts. In one of his most famous (and more readily intelligible) statements, the German philosopher Kant summed it up when he said that "human beings ought always to be treated as ends and never as means." We may have some doubts these days about who is to go to bed with whom, when, and how, but we retain a shred of morality as long as we think that the limit of all such bundling is set by the necessity of the erotic *ménageists* to treat one another as human beings. Even the most ardent advocate of recreational sex recognizes that some sort of agreed mutuality is morally obligatory. No one has yet founded a Rapist Liberation Movement.

History is, of course, full of raping, slavery, and slaughter, so one could suggest that humans have not been all that quick in recognizing this essential freedom which forbids using up folks like nonreturnable bottles. Except for militarists and mad mullahs, there are few people who would not, however, regard much of the historical record as morally reprehensible. There are also situations when we think it morally proper to "take away" freedom (prison, capital punishment), but these withdrawals of freedom always rest on some continuing acknowledgment of freedom. If the individuals are insane or incompetent, they are not punished but only confined for public safety. Even after individuals have suffered the most severe physical restrictions on liberty, we still treat them as human beings with essential dignity. Prison conditions should respect that it is human beings, not beasts of prey, who are confined. There should be a respect appropriate even for the condemned. Proper care of the body of an executed criminal is determined by a certain human dignity. It is on the basis of persistent human worth that we condemn inhumane prisons and mutilations of the most criminal of the dead.

If freedom is that-which-is-worthwhile in humankind, then any Father God who is not a mere Godfather must deal with this dignity. As the previous chapters suggested, there are lots of "superior" beings who, despite their X-ray vision, may miss this small fact about our species. Such an oversight on their part eliminates these superiors once and for all from any morally worthwhile religious tale humankind might conjure up. A religious deity story must be measured to human freedom. The religious tale should encompass both the dignity and the dilemmas of freedom.

If we assume that any single god or group of gods should pay some measured attention to our needs, then we should assess which of our endless list of gripes are appropriate for forwarding to the divine address. A god for fevers and mosquitoes makes some sense at least; a numen for herpes simplex lacks exaltedness. Before we start searching about in the universe for a superior friend, we should decide which really important problems we would like to discuss. For human beings freedom turns out to be our central cosmic claim to fame—but also our principal distress and claim for assistance. Freedom, it proves out, is in trouble with Nature, society, and itself.

The problem with freedom as a moral centerpiece is that it is so much better at telling what we should *not* do than what we should do. No slavery—black or white—no imprisonment of convenience, never humans as means. But if never as means, what is involved in the positive side of treating myself and

45

others as ends? Not only is it a puzzle on how that part is to be acted out, there is a deep suspicion that no such freedom story can acutally be written. Freedom appears to be over the heads of the folks who have been chosen to play the part.

We discovered one crisis point for freedom when we tried to fit the human square peg into Nature's curvilinear whole. From the standpoint of Nature, humans are too stupid, too sickly, and too short. If these limited biological specimens wants to stand on their dignity while facing west toward Nature, they will finally assert that dignity in some attitude of negation. I assert my dignity in the face of being dumb, dumpy, and dead at Nature's hand. There are lots of negative attitudes available to choose from when I bargain my quota of human freedom before the mightiness of Nature. I can transform Nature as much as I am able; I can defy Nature when my technology flags. I can choose to ignore Nature either in fear or defiance—saying that the natural determinants are nothing to what is really important for *human life*.

If "No!" is the ultimate response to Nature, the situation may appear very similar when we turn to society and human history. The slave receives from the careless master no greater recognition of freedom and dignity than would be received from pitiless rock or raging storm. It is conceivable that one could be the absolute slave for whom freedom in any human relation is wholly unrecognized. Society's blank eye would be in one's life like the blind eye of Nature. Knowing our essential freedom and dignity, we reject this lack of recognition; our attitude again will be negation: rebellion, defiance, withdrawal. There is a profound difference, however, between the defiance of our *social* lot and rejection of *natural* disaster. In society I *demand* recognition and redress. Nature brooks no such suit for recognition; the worst political dictator is the worst because he refuses to recognize what he ought morally to recognize: human freedom, worth and dignity.

There are moments of metaphorical fancy when the average commuter bound to a mortgage, over-committed to municipals, determined by the schedule of the MTA, caged by the demands of persisting parents, insisting spouse, and resisting adolescents may feel like the absolute slave. One may even adopt a global attitude of negation: a secret small defiance that seeps into all dealing so that the individual withdraws to the center of self away from all arrogating suburban demons. If Thoreau was correct that the majority of men (and women) live a life of "quiet desperation," then inner negation may be more extensive than one would first imagine.

For the absolute slave, the broker of quiet desperation, or humanity in final confrontation with Nature, the human subject retains freedom by vested right, but there is nothing much to be made of it. A good gnashing of teeth may be demanded in fairness to the species, but aside from adopting an attitude I cannot act out my freedom. There is no social role or action that I can take which is a proper expression of the true worth of human beings as I know it. I *recognize* that I am free; my problem is to do something with the freedom other than nodding to it.

Combining a relatively clear moral insight into the fact of human freedom with the actual achievements of freedom in Nature and history suggests that there must be a serious foul-up in the works. One could try abandoning the large world of Nature and society. Grave Stoics and gardening Epicureans adopted this strategy in various modes. The two greatest of the Stoic philosophers were an emperor, Marcus Aurelius, and a slave, Epictetus—and they both held that social position (throne or footstool) was irrelevant to anything essential about human life. The Epicureans advocate withdrawal from the great buzzing world into the serenity of the garden, a controllable acre of nature. Some interpretations of Christianity would suggest that the social world is fatally infested with original sin and a monastic cell is vastly preferable to a seat on the Exchange. Some interpretations of Freud would suggest that civilization is so full of dictated discontents that one should cultivate the psyche in a free and natural erotic retreat. An orderly retreat from the market-place of history to cultivate one's self through rational mediation, raising radishes, intoning chant, or engaging in polymorphous sex is not only a traditional life strategy but an immensely popular one in the present age. Given the mess of public life in the United States and the fact that you can charge the massage parlor to your plastic credit card, it is no wonder that inner tennis seems the key to salvation.

Attractive as the various strategies of polite retreat may be, in the long run they are, in a very precise sense, absurd. What makes these strategies bizarre is that they are grounded on the dignity of humanity in freedom but at the same time can find no earthly ground for that freedom to till. Humanity may stand on its dignity but not run with it. Society and history are rejected as unworthy because they do not measure up to the inner freedom of the self, soul, psyche, or sex. Freedom can be expressed only as retreat, withdrawal, resignation, or rejection. Real life is lived in suburban flight from unreal urban action. If one combines despair of history with disdain for nature, then human freedom retreats entirely inside one's head. In a weird inversion of common sense, nature and history are viewed as "unreal"—mere show—compared to the inner assurance and reality of one's free consciousness. Reality is only inner, and the outer world is illusion. Though it sounds like ancient metaphysics, it is the basic ideology of the "self-improvement" bookshelves where one may learn to stay Nature's sure deterioration and jog away from history.

The absurdity of peddling human freedom stuck in a world monumentally uninterested in buying is an accepted misery for a variety of existentialist philosophers and their literary fellow travelers. Humanity is portrayed expostulating from a garbage can or dictating foul epithets into a tape recorder: Samuel Beckett's *Krapp's Last Tape*, which, if the reader does not know the play, can be adequately imaged from the title. A garbage can is a limited theater for action but a good enough platform for the inexhaustible human ability to bitch. You may can me, but I will yet complain. Howling, haranguing, and abuse become both the evidence for and adequate expression of a human freedom cosmically misplaced.

Given the conflict between human dignity and the shabby historical record, joggers and existentialists are unwilling to abandon human dignity and would seek its adequate expression by some kind of running on at the feet or the mouth. The problem for the gamut of thinkers from Berne (I'm O.K.; You're O.K.) to Beckett ("I'm Krapp and how are you?") is that the basic condition of human freedom seems to suggest that any world beyond inner retreat is impossible. Human freedom requires conditions for expression that cannot be realized. One could divide such views between optimistic and pessimistic retreat masters. The pessimists like Beckett conclude that human beings are absurd, pardoxical, or—in some religious contexts—misplaced from some other world: Eden or Heaven. Optimists agree that humans may have been sent here by some cosmic postal error, but they think that if we stick to cultivating our attitudes and our artichokes we will be O.K.

So far, so bad. Let us admit that Nature is unfixable. Society and history have certainly been no great success, but surely balancing the federal budget or something will move things forward. Indeed, we might ease the pain of unrealized freedom if we were able to get the species to stick to sensible projects. Unfortunately, freedom seems to have an inner script that appears as self-contradictory as it is unavoidable.

A modestly depressing view of humanity could blame our problems on the tacky furnishing of Nature and our social tract development, but freedom is in deep trouble with itself. Freedom seems to face an impossible problem when it comes to making an effective appearance on the stage of life. There I am peeking over an Epicurean garden wall trying to decide how to exercise my freedom. Perhaps it is marriage I have in mind. After all, life is not just a bowl of radishes. I know that I am free. That means that I can choose dear Fleda Vetch next door—or Flora, Nora, or Dora. Or all of the above at once or seriatim. Or none of the above and stick with my radishes. Let us suppose that all those dear girls and vegetables are wholly cooperative; is it time to go over the wall? Sorry. The problem about settling in with any fauna or Flora in any imaginable combination is that freedom is just not the settling kind. Any decision is an excision of possibilities. Thus, to use my freedom by making a decision—even the "right" one—appears a serious constriction of freedom.

Does freedom mean everything is possible? Isn't that a bit grandiose? Everything is a lot—isn't there something in a smaller size? It is downright strange and pathetic to dither away a life on the ground that deciding to do anything specific would compromise unlimited possibility. Dostoevsky depicts just such a character in *Notes from Underground*. A nameless retired civil servant maintains his freedom *at all costs* and from the only proper place: underground. Getting out of the basement, garden, or closet would commit him to some damn thing or other.

If this fatal flaw of freedom were only the product of overheated Russian novelists, I would be inclined to dismiss it, but the same scenario keeps turning up in Clint Eastwood movies. The American fascination with westerns represents more than nostalgia for a simpler era. The western depicts in a vivid fashion the inner contrariness of human freedom. In abstract terms, a western movie is an epic of *decision against a background*. The background scenery is not just a chance to show off the virtues of Technicolor, it is essential to the meaning of the story. If there is no horizon over which the hero can

51

always ride away, then the action in the foreground loses its meaning. It is the everlasting possibility that the hero could as well be over the hills and far away that gives point and poignancy to the foreground decisions. Humanity exists between decision and dream. Decision here in the valley, dream of the ranges beyond the farthest hills. There is an unresolvable tension between decision and dream since as I decide so I forgo the dream. Yet the dream cannot be forgone: if escape over the horizon is not possible—and not a mere "theoretical" possibility—then the decision which holds me to the valley loses the background of freedom which gives it value. If I am just stuck in Gopher Gulch by natural disaster, social constraint, or personal torpor, then being there has no significant human meaning. When Shane rides over the hill in reel one and back over the hill at the fadeout, he establishes the fact that the valley exists only as a moment of decision between the horizon of all other possibilities. The horizon of unlimited freedom—so nicely photographed in the trackless expanses of western scenery—haunts the settlers and the itinerant hero. In the movies the inner tension is fictionally resolved, but in actual life the foreground/background, decision/dream tension gets only recognition, never resolution. The drifting dreamer cannot decide and settle in; he is always somewhere else, over the faraway hills.

If one needs overall characterization of our basic human longing, it would be to make decisions properly measured to the human dream of freedom. But that is deciding to settle down and skedaddle at the same time. We would like to make a decision grandiose enough to parallel our unlimited sense of ourselves: a decision measured to the mountains, not the valleys. But of course that can't be done. The inner wish, the inner *demand*, that it be done is what had led various thinkers to label humanity as *essentially* absurd, a *fundamental* paradox, an *eternal* question. Human being is itself the question which poses itself. What meaning is there for this human contraption? Humanity is a cosmic illogicality.

If religion begins with a sense of life's frustrations, one might conclude that religion tells us what to do with those unhappy facts. In a sense religions do give counsels of conduct, but the real basic question is not what we *do* but what we should *be*. It is not human *action* but human *being* that is in question in religion. I may well survey the wreck of history and decide to work against such universal woe, but the religious question is Who am I in this great struggle. Am I the despairing one, consoling my fragment of humanity? Am I the defiant one, raising my fist in anger at the bitterness of fate? How shall I be in the midst of my action? The Biblical quest is a quest for the being of human life. "How shall we be?" is the basis of religious concern. The puzzlement of human life is that while there are many actions which we might do in moral righteousness and artistic ambition, there seems no settled way to be. Our deeds, for all their worth, crumble or are overwhelmed by today's even more pressing obligation; the masterpiece of yesterday is stale and inadequate. There are always unknown mountains on the horizon.

The inescapable inner tension of humanity between being here and needing also to be there is a rich field for fantasy, neurosis, sin, and other assorted human frivolities: the fantasist absorbed in faraway fictions, the neurotic who drifts away from all decisions. Or one may bite the lip, grind the teeth, and just accept the limitations of this job, this spouse, and this late train. Be realistic! (The modern philosopher Isaiah Berlin once remarked that "Be realistic" is always the introduction to a piece of "very shoddy policy.")

The Biblical response to the dilemma of human freedom would invest limited decisions with the unlimited dimensions of our dreams of freedom. I have already noted the inveterate tendency of religious humankind to engage in "emotional overcommitment." The metaphysical saga of the Old West explains the unavoidable seduction for such supercommitments. Emotional overcommitment occurs when we accord unlimited loyalty to a limited object. My kids, my cause, my corporation, my nation—my God! It is easy enough to spy the dangers of this hyperloyalty. Exaggerated enthusiasm for a patch of the human neighborhood leads to everything from dogmatic disdain to all-out war— and usually both together. How sane it seems to caution a shot of realistic humanism.

There are three "possible" lifemanship games available depending on how one juggles the western plot between settlers and outriders. You opt for the hills, the plain, or you muddle the two. It is a clear metaphysical neurosis to drift away from all decisions whether in reality or in fantasy. But there is a deep despair in seizing on the fact of being stuck as the dominant move in the game. Stoic and Epicurean masters of realism see clearly the limited character of humanity—our limited knowledge, or feeble emotional equipment, our all too finite frame—and they enjoin us "For humanity's sake!"

to measure our dogmas, our loves, and our lives to a "generous half-acre." It is such a sensible view because it fences out the horizon of freedom which is a permanent part of the cowboy saga. Yet we fret at the short fence line and our limited life line. Neither is measured to our meaning.

The human conundrum is how to avoid an empty dreamy drifty quest which goes beyond the beyond and beyond, *ad infinitum,* and also to avoid settling for what we're stuck with, *ad finitum.* We want to decide for something sized to our freedom. There is a precise territorial characterization of this goal: we want a holy land. The horse opera philosophy of life presents the basic tension between settling in and riding off. If we could settle not just on Warner Brothers' back lot but in a *holy* land, the problem would be resolved. Settling on holy land is settling *and* somehow getting at the unlimited too.

If we want a land measured to human dignity, nothing less than a holy land seems able to suffice. "Holy land" is, in turn, a metaphor. It may be a specific piece of turf on the Jordan, the Ganges, or the Platte, but it must be a seizing of the earth, the specific, the given, the concrete *as* the holy—as more than the limited, as conjoined to, if not wholly merged with, what is as open and unbounded as our freedom. This "unboundedness" which is contained in the deed to the holy land is no longer the unboundedness of possibilites—the fact that there is always another hill over another horizon, etc., etc., etc. What is deeded in holy land is not an infinite set of travel brochures, it is all the journeys accomplished.

A set of life choices distributed among drifting, hunkering down, or setting out for the holy land does not seem too promising. All those life plans seem straight lines to futility, frustration, and despair. Drifting along on unlimited possibility detaches the dreamer from life, world, and reality; hunkering down in life, world, and reality asks us to abandon our right to a basic decision for or against life, world, and reality; hankering after the holy land with an army of Egyptians at your back and forty years of sand up ahead hardly seems a quick and easy fix. No wonder, then, that many of humankind's deep thinkers have concluded that humanity is *fundamentally* out of order.

God's Xerox

The human story is a mystery story with a sage-brush setting scripted by Samuel Beckett. We are spiritually compelled to write the poem, sing the song, play the back nine in a manner which is a full measure of our talent. And what is this great human talent? Freedom. We need a script big enough for that talent. Alas, when the script is written, it is all dialogue and no action. The hero or the heroine can shoot off a few volleys—of scatalogical verse—from any reasonably available trash can or closet, but that's it. Sometimes a script will be faked, letting incessant restlessness count as human freedom. But in that script the lead character is no character at all—all we see is the back of his head riding out of town. In the great movie western, women and gunslingers threaten the eternal rider, but he spurns the one, shoots the other, and goes off through the credits. In real life, sex or death may strike a blow for stability so that the hero or heroine abandons a fundamental restlessness for the full designation of bed, board, and Boot Hill. Yet he longs for the hills beyond!

To the commuter of common sense who wants simply to stamp out crab grass, this may seem like the sort of heavy stuff you see only in movies with subtitles: *Shane* in the Ingmar Bergman version. I repeat that it is always possible to switch off the religious track by accepting any old set of limitations. The perfect lawn, the tranquil mind, and fie on moving to a transcendental address. In the last analysis of this book, seizing the day, settling in, and detranscending are recommended. The Biblical religious problem is not against settling down; it is concerned with the *attitude* adopted by the migrant human flock. When is "settling in" true arrival and not just "settling for"? Roman philosophic strategies, like modern existential complaints, involve massive negations in which nature or society at large is rejected as an unworthy place for settlement. Where would Biblical religion have us settle: Tel Aviv, Kansas City, or the New Jerusalem?

It is difficult to be sure in modern American life whether the transgression of transcending or the sin of settling is our leading temptation. Consoled by "do it yourself" books which commend a proper vegetable patch, the average American is likely to be harangued contrarywise at a daughter's high school graduation about the need for eternal quest, searching, transcending, and generally getting on with it. Because it is the itinerant cowpoke that gets the star parts, Americans have come to believe that wandering off into the sunset is the answer to life's larger spiritual problems. For a people that invented the moving van, "going on" may seem life's last, best message. In the traditional language of religion, Americans have no trouble transcending—their problem is arriving.

America is, after all, the continuing land of migration. The Pilgrims sailed west to found a holy colony which would be a beacon unto the world. When Massachusetts would not do, Roger Williams moved on to holiness in Rhode Island. The Mormons trekked to the great Salt Lake. Hippies and their heirs and assigns thumb their way to the Golden Gate. Somewhere there is holy land, the perfect pad. Cynics might say that this American quest is not a search for blessedness but for bank accounts. It was not Spirit which led us across the oceans and the prairies but material greed. Perhaps this is true, yet there is a curious American attitude toward material goods that suggests a different scenario. If you want to see material greed, read the novels of European rural life. There one sees real avarice: the quarrel over inheritance, the right to the cherry orchard and the estates beyond. Americans, on the other hand, show a curiously transcendent attitude toward the things of this world. We are both generous and wasteful. We should take credit for giving away so much to worthy causes; we should consider how we continually use up and throw away everything from our pop bottles to our monumental architecture. Americans seem unable to fully engage with the things of their lives: homes, wives and husbands, shoes, and rock stars. We remain like the Pilgrims at sea searching for the landfall of the holy land.

Lest anyone think that the restless itch is only an American transgression like strip mining, it is worth pointing out that a philosophy of searching has the blessing of some worthy classical thinkers. The great university hero Herr Professor Doktor Faust bargains with the devil that he may have his soul if Faust ever finds anything of which he can say "Stay thou art so fair." Like Faust, we are often admonished that the quest is all: The reality of our low lot demands surpassing, overcoming, transcending, and promotion to district sales—always the cowherder, never the sodbuster.

From our picture of the basic fracture line in the human soul, there is no difficulty discovering the lure of eternal quest. "Excelsior and so on!" sounds very attractive. Even if we never arrive, we are sure to find interesting things on the way. Ponce de Leon wanted to find the Fountain of Youth and found Miami Beach instead. If I deserve the deed, the position, the lover fully measured to my worth, all human merchandise, including my body and time slot, is strictly seconds. Don Juan may recognize that in his human lineament he cuts a somewhat soggy figure, yet he gains our sympathy for his escapades because each escape from each mistress toward a boundless succession of loves is at least a passing imitation of the human spirit's search for what is better, more perfect, the holy acceptable. Elizabeth Taylor is front page "news" on the *National Enquirer* week after week. Surely she is acting out some dream scenario for supermarket shoppers.

Nietzsche, who thought God was recently deceased, commented that "man is the animal with red cheeks." Humans are ashamed of just standing around in their bodies so they blush—then they rouge up their faces to try to improve on what DNA hath wrought. Humanity just isn't good enough for our crowd; that is the reason we have taken such a keen interest in divinity. On the whole it looks like a much better position in the firm—and one which we clearly sense that we could hold better than the incumbent. The itch of transcendence so amply chronicled in the works of Zane Grey and other spiritual masters is definitely an aspiration for a better metaphysical office in the firmament.

If Nietzsche hadn't been so convinced of the demise of deity, he might have rephrased his line that mankind is the *god* with red cheeks. We act like gods who are a bit down on their luck. (Freud said that humans are "prosthetic gods.") So if the problem of this book is "Are there any gods?" the answer might well be "Yes, but they seem to have fallen on hard times." We have earlier examined the case that could be made by some awesome types (like Mother Nature) to qualify for deity. We decided that there might well be "gods" but not any to whom we could give much moral credit—celestial heavyweights, indeed, but lacking in taste. As for humanity: We have the taste for the position but we lack a line of credit.

The search for a beckoning holy land beyond the far horizon is not, then, a strange tale from the antique East. I would contend that it is played out incessantly on the silver screens and in the shoe stores of shopping malls all over America. (Why are there so many shoe stores in shopping malls? Is it the itch of transcending yesterday's fashion? Is it not proper that we continually change our marching slippers in preparation for the obscure but definitive journey?) The wayward quest for holiness, which has marked America's history from Plymouth Rock to hard rock, should remind us of the

Biblical story origins where humanity is created in the image of divinity. Our holy urge is programmed in from the first. Adam and Eve would be like Gods full and entire—that was part of the apple adventure. One should read the Bible as a confrontation between God and a reasonable facsimile thereof. In what does this image identity consist? Identity lies not in hands, toes, and lack of feathers but in the fact that God and humanity are essentially free moral agents. The proper theological questions to be posed about the human condition might be What is it like to be God's Xerox?

At first blush we might demur from this designation as theological copies. If we were even a third carbon twice removed, why can't we do our own tax returns? God by all accounts—some of which claim to be his own—is able to do all sorts of things. If I am free like a god, I am certainly not free as it seems he is to part the seas, walk on water, or speak in tongues of fire. That is surely a difference between the original and the facsimiles, but none of the so-called human limitations which could be cited as proof against divine right have any real bearing on the case.

Humankind is not free to do even small, unspectacular things, but it is wholly free to give *value* both to what can and cannot be done with ten fingers and a sharp pencil. Humans have a story to play in which the principal motif is freedom and dignity. Nothing has meaning for humanity except as it is set into that story. Any human limitation from death to drowsiness waits for humanity to assign it a value. In my pursuit of fame or sainthood, I will decide whether sleep is a blessed relief or a bothersome bore. It is not the fact of sleep that plays in the human story, it is the value. Thus, in sovereign freedom, humanity can turn aside from death, deity, or taxes and claim they play no meaningful role in the story. They occur, but they reveal nothing about the meaning of my life, which is devoted to my craft and sullen art.

One could sum up the situation of humanity by saying that in *attitude* humanity is fully divine; like the Original we have sovereign authority to assign value. Nothing constricts our moral majesty. The difference between the Original and the copies is that gods are able to carry through on their attitudes in a way that humans are not. When the Original strikes an attitude, it affects not only his values but the thing valued. Not only is death nothing to God in value—a point on which he and humans may agree wholly—it is nothing in deed either. The life of humanity and the life of God are not diminished by death; but for humanity this is an attitude and for God it is an attitude reflected in the reality of an eternal life.

God and humanity stand, then, on a parity of freedom and dignity; like a good family, they share the same values. The Father, however, lives it up according to his attitude; we cannot. Freedom applied across a universal set of off-brand merchandise is the fixed lot of humankind. We really had aspirations for Bloomingdale's but ended up in the bargain basement. When you buy seconds, they just don't quite fit. There is nothing to do except wear these togs with a certain air. Some note of casualness, of campiness, "transcends" the cut and color. *Human* freedom seems to have its natural expression in an air of negation, transcendence, and escape from limitation. Why do I wear Jordache jeans to Citicorp? Because blue jeans deny the drudgery of white-collar accountancy, and the Jordache label denies the blue-collar identity of jeans. Designer jeans are an answer to a metaphysician's dream: how to wear clothes and deny them any meaning at the same time. *Semper transcendens.*

The Biblical question to humankind is whether one finally should say Yes or No to the bargain basement selection which the Bible regards as God's creation. The "natural" human tendency—one apparently properly measured to human freedom—would be a final No. The proper "air" for life could be any one of many possible negative attitudes toward limitations: asceticism, defiance, disdain, scoffing, flight, bemusement, studied ignorance, comic casualness, campiness. If one takes a camp attitude toward life, one accepts the limitations. You live with the clothes and klutzy clutter, but by signing "A. Warhol" to life's soup can, you deny the mere mundane.

Biblical religion must understand the temptation to camp up life since it knows the deep unsettledness of human freedom. But the biblical story finally says Yes rather than No. The appropriate gesture of human freedom for our earthly pawn shop would seem to be pervasive negation, whether sensational or subtle. Biblical religion, however, urges us to find freedom in an affirmation of what is at hand. Instead of a final pose that is some off-attitude for off-brands, we are asked to take an on-attitude based on the premise that a certain affirmation of the limited can be a true gesture and full measure of human freedom.

Biblical history and the stories in the new Testament are based on the notion that in some fashion one can affirm the available merchandise, wear the raiment of mortality with a positive air after all. Christianity has become marvelously cluttered with theological speculation, conciliar formulations, and papal pronouncements on the Trinity—all of which are, I am told, much more captivating in Latin. Under all that load of elegant dialectics, there is *the* central notion of Christianity that in biblical history and the person of Jesus the limited is affirmed as full. The life of Jesus of Nazareth (a limited, historical figure) is affirmed as the fullness of a god's freedom. The claims about Jesus are not science-fiction claims about a superbeing who cleverly disguised himself as an out of work carpenter and then did all those incredible tricks, including rising from the dead. If that were the point of the New Testament tales, the basic Christian affirmation would be a simple "Wow!" What makes the story of interest is that the story of Jesus is the story of everybody faced with the problem of expressing the fullness of human dignity with a limited repertoire. The Biblical story says that the proper human attitude is a thoroughgoing affirmation of this life *and* its limits rather than a thoroughgoing negation of our lot. The problem for Biblical religion is whether we can believe in a Yes to this life.

Saints and Sexpots

It is a common assumption that religions somehow tell us about "the meaning of life." And so they do, but for the high religions there are no cheap meanings. If the Bible suggests an "affirmation" as the meaning of life, it is an ultimate Yes in the face of the manifest troubles of the world, the flesh, and whatever deviltry has yet to be reclassified as family entertainment. Given the strong case for abandoning Nature and society as inferior expressions of human morality, it is no surprise that revisionists have often read the Bible according to such assumptions. The New Testament story is a particularly likely candidate for this "moral" reading. In the natural end of death and the histroical circumstance of abandonment, Jesus refuses to accept these events as definitive of the meaning of his life. Jesus triumphs over nature and history by that refusal. In this interpretation Jesus is an exemplar—perhaps even a unique exemplar—of the spiritual triumph of humankind over the lordship of nature and history. We all are called to a similar moral heroism.

If this moral triumph is the meaning of the Christian story, then Jesus would be called "Lord" in a perfectly acceptable sense to common moral judgment. Jesus is "Lord" in the sense in which any human being from the base of freedom can rise above circumstance by declaring that human value is not determined by nature, chance, fate, or desperate men.

Moral victory over nature and fate is not to be scoffed at, but it is a mighty thin reading of the Bible. Jesus would be Lord only in the sense in which it is open to any human with enough moral stomach to command the title. One would assume that Socrates—along with a host of other ideal types—would qualify for such lordship. There is nothing so peculiar about that kind of "lordship" which should send folks scurrying about the Near East proclaiming Son of God and the other honorific labels. Big titles may boost apostolic morale, but they make poor metaphysics.

While it has certainly been a conundrum for theologians, the Jewish claim to be God's chosen people and the persistent Christian claim that Jesus is uniquely extraordinary, savior, God-in-person can scarcely be avoided if these histories are to be anything more than the available (if difficult) human refusal to have any truck with nature, chance, and station. *All* free beings deny the lordship of anything to which they do not grant moral worth. Gods and humans spurn the meaning of death. But for humankind, spurning is the best game in town. If Jesus not only spurns but actually meets death and "overcomes" it, that *is* a deed deserving coverage.

Biblical religion does not escape Nature and history; it engages them. The anguish and evil of the world are not illusions of perception; they are not public horrors from which we retreat in transcendent moral meditation and judgment. The problems of the world are "affirmed" not by some Pollyanna pretense that they are "good," but as "evils" that must be worked through. This "working through" of the trials of the world is not the task of some polytechnic pragmatist who holds that all problems can be solved with widgets and goodwill. The world described in the Biblical texts is painfully recalcitrant. Divine assistance and persistence in history is necessary; death is not cured but "lived through."

To assert the "affirmative" attitude characteristic of the Bible is far from explaining how the trick is pulled off. To understand how the Jews have "lived through" their tragic history, how Jesus lives through his death and betrayal, we must return to the fundamentals about how to be a God—and how to manage humanity.

If the Biblical story was a story of "moral" transcendence over the troubles that beset us, it would fit our ordinary divine pretensions. Human beings can (and often do) evaluate themselves as divinities down on their luck. The New Testament claim that Jesus is some sort of amalgamated divinity/humanity may not seem at all strange. Aren't we all a species of fudge between theological spirit and human flesh? We are all "gods" stuck with two feet, thirty-two teeth, and arthritis.

The big surprise is not that Jesus lets us in on the big secret that we have divine longings; it is how he reveals our humanity. Being a facsimile god is not tough for us to accept; being a genuine human is. It is shocking how this Biblical divinity traffics with *humanity*. Humanity is only a "muddy vesture of decay"—so the poet says—and as such not to be taken too seriously. If the New Testament wants to tell us that an honest-to-god God "chooses" humanity, becomes fully human, He seems to have a rather bad set of priorities. As displaced divinities, humans may be stuck with the livery of natural body and their listing in the Galactic Social Register, but we would deny our true dignity if we came to think of that extended list of limitations which we call "only being human" as fully worthy. What we refuse is not our *divine* sovereignty but our human limits. Yet the new Testament divinity accepts humanity fully—even unto death, and not an elegant one at that.

Several years ago a notorious school of Christian thinkers called "death of God" theologians arose. Unlike most theological thought these days, this theology hit the headlines. One can understand the notoriety. All those apostles, popes, and pastors had been calling our attention to God lo these many years, and then these "Christian" theologians tell us that the *theos* has dropped dead. In the long run a death of God theology would be distinctly queer, but one must give these folks credit for emphasizing the shock of the Christian story about Bethlehem and God born in a stable. The Christian notion of "God in the flesh" blocks our normal escape routes from history. Humanity in all its limitations, human history in all its mess, is accepted, engaged, "lived through." In that sense, some god dies so that humanity can be born.

According to the metaphysics of the scholars, God-becoming-man is a tough trick. True enough, but what is not said is how tough that act is for human beings to pull off. It isn't just the Holy One Blessed Be He who has problems being incarnate flesh, it is the ordinary man on the bus who is all thumbs when it comes to incarnating. Incarnating is becoming flesh, body, historical self—not just trying the costume on for size. The trick is not only difficult, it also seems distasteful and dangerous. My *body* may be short, fat, and old, but I (spirit, soul, psyche) am none of that. Incarnation sounds like the ultimate gross-out. I should *become* my body! In the traditional Christian proclamation, "God takes the form of humanity; Spirit becomes flesh." If the divinity is not just kidding around, playing costume ball, we may have to reevaluate our views of flesh and body. There is no more direct way of knowing the importance of "flesh" than through our attitudes toward sex. In sex, divine transcendence of body is well nigh impossible to maintain. If the Bible reveals humanity, is bodily humanity, sexual presence what it has in mind? That would be a surprise to Hugh Hefner and the Holy Office.

There is a good deal to be said for sex—but most folks don't regard the Bible as one of the books where it is said. All the condemnations of adultery, fornication, harlotry, and whatever they were up to in Sodom hardly make the bible read like *Penthouse Forum*. But the Bible is really interested in sex—or is interested in real sex—while the sex mags are interested in foldout fantasy. The Bible says to mankind, "You are your body." *Penthouse* says, "You are Kodachrome!" The Bible's basic incarnational, embodying, pro-sex message starts right off in Genesis when Adam and Eve are told to be fruitful and multiply—even the readers of *Playboy* probably recollect dimly how that injunction is to be accomplished. Nor do the patriarchs forget that parting shot at the gates of Paradise; their sense of "salvation" is to see their sons and grandsons unto the fourth generation. Abraham dreams of issue; Sarah is marvelously pregnant in old age, Isaac is born, taken by God, and returned; Abraham is promised that his descendants shall be as numerous as the sands on the seashore. That is the long and short of the Jewish story. Embody thyself. Thus the great modern Jewish theologian Franz Rosenzweig can make the startling statement:

> The belief [of a Jew] is not the content of a testimony, but rather the product of reproduction. The Jew, engendered by a Jew, attests his belief by continuing to procreate the Jewish people. His belief is not in something: he is himself the belief.

This Jewish view of sexually regenerated Israel has a direct relation to the notion that this Jesus is a god embodied. To understand that Christian claim, we need to look not at the characteristics of divinity but at the nature of being a body. Despite Masters and Johnson, it remains a mysterious subject. How mysterious it is can be demonstrated by pointing out how two of the great philosophers of the Western world, Plato and Hugh Hefner, have totally missed the mark on this matter.

Though it will no doubt startle the publishers, the problem with *Playboy* is that it no more understands sex than do purveyors of Platonic love. Platonic love is supposed to be a sort of spiritual communion of noble souls well above the itch and twitch of bodies.

71

Offhand that may not seem what the airbrushed bunnies have in mind. It is not an acceptance of the human body—nothing could be further from Mr. Hefner's thoughts. The last thing that *Playboy* would advocate is the human body with its sags and smells and aging and boredom. It is not real bodies that are to meet; it is ideal bodies which meet— eternally nubile, everlastingly supple, coupling endlessly without satiety in the perfect pad where no mattress shall be lumpy and no fly or phone shall buzz. *Playboy* is a true testament to the noble human spirit which refuses the mere facts of flesh and seeks something better, more ideal. The *Playboy* story is a story of eternal quest, of constant refusal to settle for second best.

Mr. Hefner and his like have not been very kind to the Bible and its spokespersons, and they are shrewd observers of the Biblical message. The Bible affirms the reality of flesh over the ideality preached by *Playboy*. In terms of the risk, excitement, searching, striving ethic of ideal sex, the Biblical picture seems absolutely dowdy. Settling down with all those grandchildren!

Marriage is obviously offensive to the *Playboy* preaching. First of all, the partners become dropouts from the sexual olympics. Surely it is better to burn with erotic ambition than to marry. The marriage idea asks human beings to do an impossible thing: on the one hand you accept this finite, fixed person and you (also finite, fixed) create in a promise of marriage a situation which no finite, fixed person could hope to achieve. Limited folks should not make unlimited commitments. Or unlimited folks (the human aspiration to divinity) should not give a lifetime guarantee on definitely wasting assets. The restless searcher—Socrates, Faust, Don Juan, Shane, and Hugh Hefner—offers a better figure for human aspiration. Judaism and Christianity offer only those neurotic Portnoys from Newark and the dreadful Deadulus from Dublin.

The offensiveness of Biblical religion is its claim about humanity, not its claim about divinity. Just as it is offensive to the sexual idealist to suggest that he or she would be better off in lifetime fidelity to a single one, so it is offensive to the religious idealist to suggest that God would exchange exclusivist vows with the Jewish people or that he would choose to definitely be one with some Nazarene woodworker. Humankind has no great trouble projecting a transcendent god and a transcending humanity; rather, it has trouble with an at-hand god and an at-hand humanity.

The religious problem is conventionally stated "What is the meaning of human life?" To understand the Biblical answer to the conventional question one has to take the question literally. What is the meaning of *human* life? What we must realize about the Biblical answer to this large question is that it is in such radical opposition to so many other philosophical and religious answers. Ascetics and bunnies might agree that there is no meaning to *human* life. Insofar as humanity is inner freedom and inner idealism wrapped in distracting or delightful flesh, the wrapper is not to be taken seriously. If bodies are mere containers, then No Deposit, No Return sex makes eminent good sense. It may be a toss-up whether the ascetic's cell or the playboy's pad is a better expression of the insignificance of human body in the true meaning of humankind. If one's basic sense of self is built on

73

any of the multiple escape mechanisms from the limitations of flesh and history, then *humanity* needs no salvation. The scientist transcending his untenured assistant professorship into the world of eternal truth, proof, and rational argument; the Stoic emperor or slave seeking a tranquil mind as the empire collapses; the Epicurean gardener walled into a quietude of nature while the great world rages without; the playboy/playgirl abandoning the cares of office in the timeless moment of erotic bliss—all these good folk, if they adopt their escape mechanism as *the* meaning of human life, have decided that mere humanity either cannot or ought not be saved. What is shocking about the Bible is that it suggests a salvation for *humankind* while its deity chooses *human history*.

The Bible makes two mistakes from the standpoint of the transcenders: It wants to save what is so obviously not worth salvage, and it removes "salvation" from human action. If the meaning of life can be defined in terms of my paticipation in the quest of science, the tranquilty of a cultivated mind or a cultivated "pleasure" garden, these are salvations which are more or less within my grasp. But saving the human body, saving sheer humanity and its shabby history, is not within our grasp. "Salvation" lies in actively abandoning the limitations which body, history, and humanity suggest in favor of timeless rationality or sexuality.

Saving the body is not a trick for resurrectionists. The Bible says that this finite body, this limited history, is inherently an ingredient of the divine. Living this life in this overweight body is *already* living eternal life. Christian resurrection offers not a continuation of what a Platonist already regards as a second-rate state; resurrection is the assertion that the supposed limitation of a *human* life is *already* overcome. Resurrection in Christianity does not mean *continuation* of the limited; it means *fulfillment* of the limited. My three score and ten is all the life that I have—there is no "to be continued" marker on the gravestone. In Christianity every death is a definitive death, and one can legitimately mourn at the shortness of it all. What Christianity says in the notion of resurrection is that this finite and definitive life is not continued but amplified. It is as if life were one tune and when it is done that is the tune—there is no second movement. But God orchestrates life's jingle into eternity; hence the importance of *this* life for "heaven" or "hell." If you compose a dumb song you are stuck with it. An eternity of Bach may be heaven, but Chubby Checker is another matter.

The figure of Jesus as in-fleshed divinity affirms the reality of sheer/mere humanity. Humanity is not the wrapper of divinity; we are told that this human is God all in all, whole in whole. If one believes in such an at-onement of divinity and mere human history, then in that life the apparent limitation of flesh and bone is overcome. By seizing on my day, my life, my history, I imitate the definitive choice which God makes of human life.

Whether or not Biblical theology is unique, its "anthropology" certainly is. Biblical religion takes human history, human life, human body with more positive seriousness than they seem to deserve. The human story from Genesis to Judgment is truly human *and* truly a story. It is easy enough to have one or the other but not both. We do tell stories—but they are stories fit for higher-order species:

75

heroes and gods. This life is the struggle of these superhumans to assert moral courage and ideal values in shabby circumstances. But for ordinary humanity, it is like the existentialist protagonist who says, "In life nothing happens." For run-of-the-mill existence there is no story. In the Biblical view it is precisely in the everyday existence that the story is found. That story is "salvation" from "sin" through "love."

9

A Good Word for Sin

Before supplicants could approach the sacred mysteries of the great temple of Delphi, they passed under a portal with the inscription "Know thyself." That is proper advice for advancing toward gods and their oracles. "Who am I?" "What is human reality?" would appear to be the fundamental questions for our life. Am I the child and heir of benevolent powers or the orphan of a casual cosmic accident? "What is humanity?" can be given focus by finding where we fit into the array of other occupiers of the universe: molecules, mollusks, and divinities (real or imagined). As we assay the other occupants (or empty slots), we determine who and what we are and decide on the life appropriate to our kind. We make a fundamental life choice (no matter how inarticulate and hidden) on how we fit in the scheme of cosmic things.

It would seem that the array of life choices is indefinitely complex, variegated without end. Should I listen to the Pope or Pink Floyd in laying out a life plan? A bit of consideration reveals, however, a most restricted set of choices below the dazzling surface of the world-dispersed spiritual nostrums. There is a plausible argument that the number of *basic* choices should be sharply limited. If faiths and philosophies were as various as first appears, then making a basic life choice would be a task only for encyclopedists. Until one had scholarshipped through the array, one would have no business deciding on a life to be led. While a basic argument of this book has been that life begins in frustration, the frustration of footnotes is not what it had in mind.

At the religious level, the life question is fundamentally very simple despite the richness of ritual and philosophy that may follow. All religions want to know whether humans *fit* in the available universe. Is this alien territory where we should be on guard or is it friendly land where we may—at least ultimately—expect support from the proprietor? If we judge that humanity is misplaced in the current location, then there may follow an array of analyses and conjectures about what to do now and next. Perhaps this dazzling display of beauty and destruction is all illusion behind which lies a better world. If I think there is a way to that better world, I may use whatever plausible spiritual travel techniques are suggested. Or I may conclude that the better world is only an unreachable ideal. Should I strive to make the local territory at least a first approximation or adopt an air of quiet acquiesence to the transient pleasures of the day? Around these basic considerations and their cousins, great religions and noble philosophies have grown in splendor. Biblical religion faces the same issue but makes a very strange move. Rather

than judge this world in the light of a real or ideal
other (better) world, Biblical religion seeks to understand humanity in the world at hand. Biblical religion is uniquely "world-affirming." That formula
must be carefully understood, however, in relation
to other spiritual views which could be regarded as
world-affirming or world-denying.

There is a great tradition in which an "inner" self
is affirmed and the given world denied. As has been
pointed out, Stoics, Epicureans, Plato, and *Playboy*
are all world-denying in their special ways. Something more rational, more controllable, more ideal,
more sexy is desired than the at-hand world pro-
vides. The actual practical course from such idealiz-
ing is infinitely complex. Playboys and Platonists
may withdraw to an appropriate pad, erotic or eru-
dite as the case may be. Or they may issue forth
from their cave of ideality into the poor old shabby
world and seek to shape it up according to plan. In
an ironic fashion the religion of monastic retreat and
the cult of technological improvement meet coming
in opposite directions through the same door.

If one chooses neither to retreat from the world
nor to spruce it up to better standards, what is the
alternative? What would it mean to "affirm the
world"? One might imagine an attitude of quietude
and acceptance. It would have to be a special sort of
acceptance, however, not the quietude of despair.
"What comes will come (sigh!)." (I recall a *New
Yorker* cartoon in which two obviously well-to-do
types are having a conversation. *She:* "Millicent has
decided to accept the world." *He:* "By gad, she had
better!") The problem is not resigned acceptance
and acquiesence, it is *affirming*. To affirm the world
is to involve oneself in the world in some obviously

positive fashion. We have already said enough
about the basic position of human freedom and
dignity to make it clear that "accepting the world" is
not denying human freedom. One could "accept"
the world in the sense of acquiescing to its basic
physics. But that won't quite do for human
freedom; a free being affirms what shares a free life.
Molecules do not. Pompous as it seems, we are not
likely to affirm something that isn't going to nod in
return. "I said hello and got not even a 'by your
leave.'" If the essence of humanity is freedom, then
affirming "who I am" is affirming this freedom.
Affirming the world is recognizing the world as a
proper place for this freedom. To the extent that
"nonhuman" reality is judged basically "mechani-
cal," "unresponsive," "mute," that realm is not
affirmed. I withdraw from the nonhuman or I seek
to transform it into humanized shape. My free hand
is impressed on the harsh granite as unforgiving
stone becomes human art.

The previous chapter argued that Biblical religion—despite a ferocious tradition of seeming
world denial by assorted Calvinist ministers and
desert monks—is a world-affirming religion.
(World-affirming is a religious position which Jews
find much more plausible than Christians.) The
trick for Biblical religion is to find out how it is done.
How can these featherless bipeds, limping along in
their bit of dignity, bring themselves to say "Yes" to
a world which seems most uninterested in this
"Yes"? (It seems equally deaf to "No," but existentialists feel more authentic for having said it.)

A catechetical statement of world-affirming is
found in Genesis. Unlike lots of other deities, such
as Plato's, the God of Genesis is a thoroughgoing

creator. He is not a shaper-upper who, having found some immemorial goo, decides to shape it up as best he can. Plato says that in creation "reason persuades necessity"; Plato's god does the best he can in molding the initial irrational chaos. But we all know that reason always has a tough time persuading anything, and Plato's god is only somewhat better than your average university president. The result is that while Plato's cosmos is a good deal tidier than the previous chaos, it is only so-so. Even god cannot wholly affirm it. It is just his best effort. Not so with the God of Genesis, who makes a considerable claim when he looks down and declares his handiwork not only "good" but on second thought "very good." The world in the Bible story is not, then, God's best imitation of a good order; it is wholly affirmed by this God. Plato's god has no "problem of evil"; he can blame it on defective material. The Biblical God is wholly responsible.

It is hard to buy the Biblical claim of a very good world on simple evidence, and the Bible itself does not read at all like Wordsworth. Wordsworth, when he is not meditating over daffodils and little girls who have drowned in the bogs, detects in Nature a "something far more deeply interfused which is the light of setting suns." Wordsworth and a whole line of nature poets are quite willing to see Nature as the expression of a deeper moral power. They are "world-affirming," at least as long as the world to be affirmed has a proper number of lakes and rills. Whatever Biblical religion may be, it certainly is not Wordsworthian. The age of pastoral poetry ended with Adam and Eve. Wordsworth would have been the perfect poet for Paradise where the Something more deeply interfused was fusing out all over.

Unhappily, after the Fall, Nature turned a rather bleak cheek to humankind. This *après-le-Fall* Biblical picture of the world seems much more in tune with perceived reality than does the enthusiasm of nature poets. Poets may be able to "affirm" the world in certain spectacular moments like sunsets, waterfalls, and stranded daisies, but these are rather Epicurean affirmations—affirmations of a strictly limited garden of transcendental delights. The real problem is affirming that world which, Wordsworth says in a more trenchant mood, is "too much with us."

To understand how humanity can affirm in a fallen world, we will have to understand our fall and fault. This book hopes overall to make the notion of God tolerable for conversation outside funeral services. It is not a trendy task. If we now turn to the notion of "sin," things are unlikely to improve. One could probably get even money on which notion is more out of date—"God" or "sin." But there is no way to tell the Bible story without talking about sin. The prophets are constantly berating the Israelites about their transgressions, and the traditional New Testament story is that Jesus "saves" from "sin." No sin, no savior, no story at all. So a few good words about sin.

The first thing that needs to be said about sin is that it is not mere moral indiscretion. Even more specifically, sin is not sex. There were moments in my education from the Irish Christian Brothers when I had the distinct impression that the entire point of the creation of the sun, the moon, and stars, the journeys of the patriarchs, the flight out of Egypt, the proclamations of the prophets, the New Testament, and the pageant of the Popes was to stamp out smooching. Never has so much earnestness been devoted to so little effect.

There is a connection between sin and moral fault—even sexual moral faults, of which I hope there still remain a few. But the connection is not one of identity. Sin is not a matter of specific larcenies, lies, and leers. We are not interested in the retail faults of the race (many as they may be); we are interested in a wholesale attitude which lies beneath all these petty crimes and major misdemeanors. Sin is not the acts done; it is the final "spirit" of the acts. In its classic formulation sin is spiritual presumption, not a performance.

The sin of Eve and her helpmate is not an inherently wicked deed. Eating apples has not since had such drastic consequences. The issue between God and our prime parents was who (or what) were these newly crafted beings: animals, gods, "humans." The decision for sin is not first a decision for bad actions; it is the wrong decision about who I am. There is obviously a subtle connection between what we *are* and what we *do*, yet the two issues are distinct. Character is the summation of many actions, but it is a summation that goes beyond simply summing the series. A life of thievery will surely make a thief, but if I ask forgiveness at the end then I am a different person than the one who dies in anger and despair. There was something else going on in this person all along that was hidden until that last confession and that calls for a reassessment of the whole.

Who am I is more revealed in the mood of actions than in the actions themselves. Actions spring from moods, and many actions have the appearance of similar shape and value. If I give to the college of my

83

choice from annoyance at the IRS or gratitude for professional tutelage, in either case the act is the same and contributes to the social good. Moods, of course, have tendencies to action. The angry person is a difficult companion—unless of course the anger is turned inward and externalized as controlled benevolence. If sin is a mistake about who I am and this mistake is revealed in mood or attitude, what shall we say about Adam and Eve? The traditional description of the first fault is that it was "pride." These first humans forgot who they were and would be gods, not God's special creatures. Pride is not an action but an attitude. Eating an apple *in pride*—if that sets the human fashion—may well be sufficient to initiate the catastrophe of human history.

In an earlier chapter we outlined a basic Wild West mystery story for the human cast of characters. In that world of settled valleys and beckoning mountains, what is the proper answer to "Who am I?" What is the mood for these mountains? Life in this story is always "decision against a background." In the at-hand world of the valley, one commits marriage and murder. But decisions in the valley are always haunted by the far horizon. The horizon is freedom; it is the ever-present reality which gives point and poignancy to my decisions in the gulch. If I merely stuck in the valley, then my actions are what they are, but the meaning of my life changes. The eternal rider may perform the same actions, but the life is different.

If the first problem for our first parents (and for us) is "Who are we?" how should that question be answered in the light of the cowboy scenario? A first analysis of the situation may suggest that the question is utterly unanswerable because the human race has incurable metaphysical schizophrenia. We are faced with an inner demand to be a certain sort which we seem quite incapable of realizing. We have the demand of freedom—the ever-present measure of the mountains—but if I pursue that life; nothing is ever settled; *I* am never settled. "Who am I" will never be settled because *I* am always "over the hills and far away." The only adequate life is incessant flight.

Freedom opens up a world of possibility. Does freedom then demand we should be *all sorts of different persons.* Suppose at the end of *Shane*, after Alan Ladd takes care of Jack Palance, he decides to run off with Jean Arthur and sell Brandon de Wilde to the Indians. Why not? We have emphasized the absolute ground of freedom and possibility. Isn't Ladd becoming all too predictable—always saving maidens from villains with a three-day growth of beard? To assert the freedom script, he should show off the infinite variability and plasticity of human action.

Can one combine a demand for open freedom with our sense that Alan Ladd ought to *be* somebody? As an actor, Alan Ladd could and did play everything from sadistic killers to heroes like Shane. If that had been his real life—one day a hero, the next day a hood—we would have looked for some deep psychic link for these disparate characters. To be a person is to be *some* person; to be free is to use that freedom to be some person, not to turn over in infinite variety all the ways of life. That script is *Shane* written by the Marquis de Sade.

Given humanity's paradoxical setting, one might now say that sin is not so much a problem of what *sort* of person I shall be, but whether I can be a person *at all*. If we choose a certain course of action as our self-definition, how will we come to terms with the horizon of freedom? Two modes present themselves. We choose in depair or choose in pride. To choose the self in despair is to accept (and curse) the factors that confine us to the settler's valley. We choose, we must choose—only in the valley are there choices and not escapes—but we chafe at the restricted life that is thus defined. On the other hand, we choose in pride—like a God—and think that our decision here and now encompasses the full range of possible lives. In the various strategies of limitation which have been set forth in this analysis, such as Epicureanism and Stoicism, it is not clear whether these are to be adopted in pride or despair. When Candide is urged to "cultivate his garden," it is after the wreck of his Panglossian hopes to improve the world. But one could also choose limitation as a gesture of self-righteous assurance and pride. My world, my garden, my internal peace of mind is the only worthy life. The Bible directs us to choose in *faith*. We act in the valley, procreate this Israel, just these sons and daughters, but this worldly act is opened beyond itself to the holy and fulfilled.

The human problem is to be free and to be somebody at the same time. I can certainly be free as an *actor:* one who performs actions or one who performs roles. As an *actor* my actions and my parts are always open and infinitely plastic. If there is a solution to the human conundrum, it will be to discover a sense of being free which is not the freedom of the actor. The human issue is to be a character, not a character actor. The God of traditional theology manages this feat. In virtue of his most impressive godliness, he is free to act in all ranges of the remotest possibility. At the same time, he is supposedly somebody. If he were just a collection of possibilities, he wouldn't be somebody at all; he would be a blank slate on which universes get scribbled from time to time. But if he is a decent God, then there is a core of will, personality, character—he is somebody. St. Paul may have been all things to all men, but God should be something steadier.

Let us call God "a freedom somebody." I choose this odd locution to differentiate a god from any one of us. We are all free somebodies in the sense that we have other possibilities ahead us—if we choose. God, on the other hand, encompasses all possibilities; he is freedom realized, not merely beckoning in future choice. The theological issue is whether or not "a freedom somebody" is possible. If Shane can pull it off, then Alan Ladd is Lord. Resolution of the predicament of settling in and being free is the acheivement of real star status. Mankind would become the *theos* we have been searching for not only in aspiration and presumption but *de facto*, the real thing. I assume that such resolutions of the human puzzle are only the stuff of Paramount Pictures. Human beings are not stars (cosmic or otherwise) once the kliegs are off.

The Bible says that we can win through to being legitimate (and free) somebodies by entering into some genuine direct relation with God—the freedom somebody. The relation is more than aesthetic admiration; religion is not a spectator sport. Somehow our wayward and contrary struggles to have a meaning for my life, be a somebody, are grounded in our relations to God. Sin is a refusal to play (or play fair) in the game of freedom. To play in this game we must accept a set of theological rules. In this game we are necessarily involved with godliness. The name of the game is "Make a Life." Act, re-collect, and reposition acts so that at the end life has been more than a tourist's itinerary. Winning the game is being somebody. Losing is refusing to be somebody or faking it. For humans, being *somebody* seems to require being a definite or "restricted" somebody. We play this game in the valley. But isn't being a "restricted" somebody one of the losing moves? We have to *ground* life; can it be grounded in something "beyond" in a larger meaning?

What does it mean to "ground your life"? The meaning of your (limited) life can be grounded not just in what you can accomplish before the undertaker but also in another's life. We might ground the meaning of our life in our children or our troops. We pour out all that we are into their persons and characters. Our life expands beyond itself into their lives; life is grounded in another. If we could ground our life decision to be somebody in an unlimited other, then we would win this life game of freedom. We would expend our life with all its necessary limitations and imperfections, but its final *meaning* would be grounded in another who is without such limitations. That scenario is the basic Biblical script.

Adam and Eve found themselves in a setting not of their choosing, but it was "good," yea "very good" according to the owner and manager. Fine. But for all its special delights, this setting could not answer the questions "Who am I? What are we?"

One thing they did know: They were free some-
things because they could perform a strange act—
they could choose. They had been admonished not
to choose apples. Perhaps it would have been nice
to have had something more important to ponder,
but it is the choosing, not the choice, that is the
issue. Eating the apple turns out to be a cataclysmic
consequence because of the self that is chosen in
this choice. As we choose acts, we also choose the
self we would be in the act. The challenge to Adam
and Eve is this: as free, what sort of *person* will you
be? In their big test, Adam and Eve exercise their
freedom to establish the world as *theirs*. The gift of
the Other is taken as ours by choice and appropria-
tion. The apple, rightfully the Other's, restricted as
his and surrounded by admonition, is seized as ours
by right.

The original sin is not an act of "thievery" or mere
disobedience; it is a fundamental choice about human being. Our primal parents played to type: They
exercised freedom to dominate, to appropriate a
world that should have been to them a gift. To
ignore the *gift* of the world and act as if it were
personal property is to dominate like gods. Original
sin is primal sin; it is the exercise of legitimate freedom as if we were gods rather than free creatures in
the gift of the world. The original choice is to establish human being as a false god. And so it has been
with the historical record.

Humanity continues in the delights of sin by
playing this "domination" scenario in everyday life
and soap opera. The solution to this persistence of
godlike choice would be to realize again that the
world is best defined as "the-gift-of-an-other."

Salvation from sin is moving out of the "let's-play-God" and dominate our world (or, the converse, despair at our world because it is not up to our (divine!) standards). The short formula for salvation is love. Love is accepting the other as gift; it is giving self to the one who gives.

10

Love Thy Neighbor and Other Implausible Notions

The Bible is one of the more implausible books on the best-seller list. To any junior high school science teacher it obviously poses lots of problems. What were the astronomical effects of the sun stopping so that Joshua could finish off Jericho by daylight? It is not only showstoppers that are a problem; all that ferocious war poetry hardly conforms to the UN charter. And, in all honesty, it is often pretty dull reading. All those "begats." There are Bible enthusiasts who regard the whole lot as equally and infinitely valuable. The Good Lord carefully selected every preposition and filled it with cosmic meaning. How interesting that Esau was a hairy man! Text worship, however, denies the Bible the capacity to interpret itself. Any author, even a divine one, has a plot that carries the sense of the whole. When in doubt about a footnote, it is advisable to understand it in terms of the main point. The main point of the Bible is not the production of the Bible but the central tale that it tells in a variety of picturesque ways. The central themes of the Bible earn its place on the

Great Book List. Creation, the relation of human and divine life, sin, salvation, judgment: those are perennial best-sellers. To read the Bible correctly and to make its religion more than an exercise in willful belief, one has to get at the reasons why Creation et al. are compelling themes.

While much of the Bible may seem scientifically outrageous and morally antique, the difficulty of managing weddings and burials has preserved some of the text in common use. One of the more admired messages is the advice about loving one's neighbor. Having invited one's dubious relations to a family wedding, it is consoling to hear the preacher reminding them to love one another. Loving the neighbor has come to be the centerpiece of Christianity not only by those who are embarrassed by any theological machinery but by deep theologians who see this injunction as a piece of a revolutionary social gospel. Centering on "neighbor" is not without New Testament justification. On being asked to sum up the Law and the Prophets, Jesus concludes with "love thy neighbor as thyself."

There are two immense problems with this conventional distillation of the Law and the Prophets. In the first place it is not *exactly* what Jesus said; in the second place it may have an implausibility deeper than Joshua calling the sun to a sudden halt. Jesus said that one could boil the Bible down to "Thou shalt love the Lord thy God with thy whole soul and thy whole mind" and *then* "thou shalt love thy neighbor as thyself." Given the obsessive interest in God through the other sixty-six books of the Bible, it is unlikely that one should ignore the first and longer injunction as so much elevating puffery. The second problem with "Love thy neighbor" is that it turns out on examination to be one of those innocent injunctions like "Be yourself" which became invitations to metaphysical disaster. The last chapter examined the problem of "being yourself," and it proved to be surprisingly complicated. "Love thy neighbor" proves equally problematic and also involves theological relief. The two parts of Jesus' injunction are, in fact, not separable.

If one asks about the meaning of life, that is the kind of question which religions purport to answer. The meaning of this strange tangle of life appears to be improbably complicated. We need a story up to our aspirations. We need a cosmic narrative but manage only cosmetics. One way to extend the self would be to ground the meaning of our person in some other. Thus, the meaning of our life would be given wider, broader extent; more in keeping with its expansive worth. The passion for parenting and poetry comes from the demand for an expanded self as we see ourselves live in others and our deathless sonnets.

At this point, the notion of loving thy neighbor begins to have cogency. Our lives expand toward a proper breadth of meaning as we ground them not in our own self-absorbing activities but in the lives of our neighbors. If we choose benevolence toward the folks down the block, we will already have abandoned a number of life-meaning strategies. Stoics think life's value is found in theoretical meditation. Neighbors are not be trusted with your life meaning. Epicureans might allow you to loan a lawn mower, but safety lies in the self-sufficiency of your own garden. It has been argued that some far Eastern religions with their radical discounting of the external world are not likely to be all that interested in the local neighborhood of a second-rate cosmos. In short, there are lots of arguments for tranquility that would caution against grounding one's life in the life of another. I hardly trust myself, why should I trust *you!*

Despite such sober words of ultimate caution, there is a presumption for doing good to thy neighbor that has come to pervade the welfare democracies of the Western world. I would not for a moment wish to see it reversed. Before one gets to the deep predicaments of loving stablemates, confidants, and distant nephews, one should point out that much of our fellow feeling probably is not *loving* the neighbor at all. Our "charitable" impulses may well be based on sterner stuff. Stable community may suggest that we help out the losers lest they disturb the social order. We may have a legitimate aesthetic distaste for the shabbiness of disease and distress. Our station may carry with it a need to appear magnanimous. And so on. In all of these alternative motives, we are not seeking to ground the meaning of our life in a neighbor. It is only when we act on humanity's infinite presumptions that we turn toward the other to ground our meaning. If I *love* my neighbor, the relation between the other life and my life becomes a single issue. I want my life expanded in and through the other; thus, in some odd sense I have to "find" my life in that life. Love is a good enough name for that strange relation of persons. Love, unlike reasoned philanthropy, fails to keep a proper distance. In reasoned philanthropy we help as best we can. Alas, the poor chap couldn't make it even with our best efforts. Shame. But, when I *love* my neighbors their suffering is mine, their life mine, their death mine. It may make some sense to "lay down my life for my friend," but that seems a bit much even for the Boy Scouts.

The injunction "love thy neighbor"—particularly in the context of all the other excitements of the Biblical story—must be something more than a general mail appeal for the Red Cross. If we suppose that loving our neighbor is the solution to a meaning for our lives, would it work? Would it work without the first part of Jesus' injunction about the Lord thy God? Can we give meaning to our lives on the "horizontal"—just loving away at the neighbor? Or is there some necessary "vertical" dimension to the referent of the Our Father?

A simple suspicion that we won't ground our aspirations to both be somebody and be "unlimited" can be derived from the obvious fact that our neighbors are in the same predicament as ourselves. We need them to expand our life and they need us to expand their life. We seek to ground our aspirations to the freedom script in folks who cannot themselves act out that script. Like a community of the blind, we may well pool our sense of the world, but we will never see it. Americans are friendly people; they are not unimpressed with finding a life meaning in friends and lovers. What is noteworthy is how unsatisfactory this quest for meaning-in-another has become. The divorce courts testify to our belief in marriage but its uncertain success. We believe in the proper partner, psychiatrist, or diet counselor, but we seem unable to really settle on any one for sure. The essential incapacity of others relative to our (legitimate) aspiration may explain the statistics on instability. We need a "divine" other.

Earlier we discussed infralapsarian substitutionary theology. When teenagers or their elders adulate the stars of rock and roll, the silver screen, or the playing field, they seek to live their lives in another, in the star if not exactly in Heaven. The impulse is now fully explainable: How shall we ground our life in a life which is worthy of that inner sense of meaning? Why, for realism's sake, don't teens simply recognize their station in life (humble enough but decent) and stop having aspirations to glory! Even teens have immortal longings. Humans apparently cannot come to terms with simple reality; they all want to be God or Madonna. If I become the "adoring" fan, if I pour out my life and my pay packet for the Star, then her life and my life become mystically one. (This actually works both ways. Fans secretly realize that the rock star is their creation, grown great, yea even unto a platinum record, by the mass effect of continuing loyalty.)

Despite the stern warnings of the great spiritual masters, humanity does seem to continue on its wayward career of overinvesting emotional capital without an adequate tax write-off. We love wives, husbands, children, rock stars, and even neighbors in a manner highly dangerous to a tranquil mind. Our (free) life has been bound over to all these others so that it is not clear that when our life story is told it will be ours. We were interested in loving these irrational neighbors because it seemed that it might be an answer to how to lead a life which had a scope beyond the vegetable patch. Our life would be their life; it would extend through other lives and not be so geographically cramped or so full of reading books on philosophy. But the others seem so monumentally uncooperative. Oh yes, as children and lovers they do partly live our life—they understand our wishes, needs, views, and tastes in California wines. But they play the part so badly! It is my life story but they have cast Bette Davis (or Bette Midler) in the lead. Great saints and lovers have certainly seen the final failure and misunderstanding of their cause in the most ardent of their disciples. Church history may be a case in point.

Perchance you find the perfect lover and the truthful disciple. Now you will discover that there are problems on *your* side. We suspect the disabilities of the beloved, we know our own. The relation of parent to child is perhaps the most striking. We create them, love them, pledge our life to sustain them, we abandon them. This abandonment has been known since the moment of conception as we rationally project our death. We do not consider our children in their old age and distress. Are they not still our children? The heart cries out to console them in their desolation. How bizarre! Long since dead, we are obsessed with this picture of loving these aged wrecks who are (were) our children. Too much rationality applied by loving couples to giving birth may well convince them that it ventures too much. We would give all to the children, but common sense projects persistent, continual, and final failure. Prudent control of births is laudable; ultimate prudence, however, may suggest that it is better not to get started at all.

When it comes to loving thy neighbor, a bit of sobriety would suggest that neither me nor thee are quite up to it. If love is living life in another, then morally I cannot so command your life or commend my life. Just when you had counted on my sterling performance in your big scene I abandon the whole project for some distraction like death. Enough meditation on the distresses of domestic life leads straight back to a philosophy of limited risk. The modern love story is not living in the life of another; it will be just living in.

The muddle of loving is what traditional theologians call the problem of salvation. How can we give over our fate, happiness, and autobiography rights to anyone else? This is *my* story. If I am obsessed with *my* story in the fashion of the self-help books, then salvation is distasteful because salvation *comes from another*. In the older language it was "grace," a gift, something gratuitous. If the modern world seems particularly deaf to hymn singing, it may be because we are so convinced that the only story worth telling is self-scripted. We have accepted a virulent version of the "freedom is *my* story" scenario. Accepting grace or Grace is not acceptable. Loving neighbor or live-in is not possible—at least under the stronger versions of love—because it would be witless, wicked, and unsanitary to give my life over to another. We can accept social security and farm price supports, but that isn't love, it's social calculation.

Loving thy neighbor is a step in the proper direction for "solving" our basic life enigma. Our inner sense of worth expands beyond a narrow life. It finds expression in something larger: comrades, country, cause. To make the gesture measured to our meaning, we invest our full worth, our life savings. But for all that we have a large intention, our means are meager. I invest the whole of my human, all too human capital with a distinct sense that it falls desperately short. On top of that, the human, all too human firm in which I have made this ultimate investment is in deep trouble. Meager meets meager. In the roundelay of loving the neighbor, I am not as good as a lover nor are you as a neighbor that we can have any confidence in the transaction. What we need in our wounded condition is a neighbor in whom we can invest, who is large enough for the intent of our gesture, who can make more of it than we know how.

After admonishing us to love thy neighbor, Jesus is asked, "Who is my neighbor?" He then tells perhaps the most famous parable in the New Testament: that of the Good Samaritan. A luckless traveler on the way from Jerusalem to Jericho is set upon by robbers and left wounded by the side of the road. In succession, various publicly pious officials come by but hurry on to their business without offering assistance. Finally an "outsider," a Samaritan, comes by. He binds the traveler's wounds, brings him to an inn, and pledges to pay for all necessary care.

Who is the neighbor? The normal interpretation is the unfortunate traveler who we are counseled to assist. But this is not what the parable says. "Who was neighbor unto him who fell among thieves?" asks Jesus. The Samaritan, of course, say his inquisitors. So? Love thy neighbor. According to the parable it is the Samaritan who picks you up from the side of the road! That is the one I am supposed to love? Gosh, I thought it was that crabby Mrs. G. who lives in the next apartment. A literal interpretation of the parable would be that the neighbor to be loved *first* is the one who saves us from the wreck of our life journey. *That* neighbor is fully worth the intent of my inner dignity and evidently knows how to bind my wounds and correct the defects of my imperfect good intentions. Loving the neighbor starts with finding a lover properly measured to our freedom; this would be a "savior" to whom we could fully entrust the meaning of our life. If our neighborly gesture, well intentioned however weak, can be bound into health by the Good Samaritan, then it might be safe enough to spread our own neighborliness around to unsuspecting friends and relations. In the Biblical story, we can set about loving after we "solve" the infirmities of human loving. For this we need salvation.

11

All Others Pay Cash

The Bible is a book of salvation. Even if you skip over the last part, it seems clear that the Jews were waiting for something better to happen to them than the arrival of the Persians and the Romans. God should have had something happier in mind for a chosen people. Whatever else Christianity may be, it seems on its face clearly to be a religion which preaches salvation and a savior. Before one becomes instantly bored with that idea, it is important to note that most other significant spiritual contenders not only don't preach salvation, in some cases they positively dislike it. Islam is a case in point. Islam means "surrender"; there is no God but Allah and there you are! Muslims find the Christian notion of a savior demeaning both to the saver and the saved. God can accomplish his ends for humanity without complex metaphysical gyrations, and dependence on a savior would devalue the moral independence and fortitude of the intended clients. Human folks ought to stand on their own two bare feet and get on with saving themselves.

Buddha is not a savior, he is the Enlightened One. He has seen the truths of human life, and he offers the Noble Eightfold Path as a guide to similar enlightenment and release from suffering. In later Buddhism, there are great ones who, having attained Buddhahood, postpone Nirvana to stay around and help the unenlightened. These "Bodhisattvas" are inspired and compassionate teachers of Enlightenment but they are not saviors. The great Chinese spiritual teachings follow the rubrics of moral law and enlightenment. They face directly toward the human reader and suggest that he act more propitiously (Confucius) or that he consider more deeply the ways of the heavens and the earth (Taoism). Hinduism is a splendid polytheism in which various gods and goddesses intervene to accomplish temporal and spiritual ends for struggling humankind, but in the long run Hinduism also seems to be a religion of Enlightenment, not Salvation. The individual adherent orders his life and thought toward eternal bliss without the need of radical reconstruction from some saving spirit. While this is a *very* crude characterization of the world's major spiritual traditions, it is accurate enough to point up the quite peculiar stress on salvation in the Bible.

The world's other religious traditions are traditions of Moral Correction or Spiritual Enlightenment. For enlightenment or morality one needs teachers, not saviors. The distinction is crucial. On the whole, religions of morality or enlightenment are much more palatable to contemporary American taste. They have two distinct advantages over the Biblical tradition. In the first place they appear to be do-it-yourself spiritualities. This conforms to an

American taste for independence and self-reliance. Self-help is what we seek in the latest nonfiction remainder list. Although great teachers are valuable in these traditions, they are also dispensable, and one can be self-taught. One cannot be self-saved in the Biblical story. The second advantage of religions of enlightenment and morality is that they can dispense with most theological machinery. If there are Gods at all—and in Buddhism there appear to be none—then their role is either as helpful (but dispensable) teachers or as ideals and exemplars. The truth is in the teaching, not in the teacher-savior.

Americans like to believe they are self-made. Rugged individualism, hard work, and Yankee cunning have conspired to make a raw continent an everlasting "bread machine" of wealth and comfort. The preacher piously advised the New England farmer on his cultivated field: "What you and God have accomplished!" The farmer replied, "You should have seen it when only God was working the field." If this metaphor of "self-made" is truly a defining character, Americans will have no need for an outside maker or an external savior.

Sacred texts which are regarded as testaments of enlightenment or correction need no gods, so pastors who are embarrassed by supernatural machinery may wish to recut the Bible on these interpretations. In that view, the Bible is recast with *teachers:* prophets, assistant prophets, associate prophets, and one (at least) holder of a Heavenly Endowed Chair. The new cast of moral and metaphysical faculty delivers a variety of noble thoughts on how to live a life and some pungent descriptions of how things turn out when you don't pay attention in Sunday school. The leading actors of the Bible are teachers, not saviors. Salvation is up to you in the pew.

No doubt there is a lot of worthwhile moral advice in the Bible. I can't say that I think it as good as *The Nichomachean Ethics* or Jane Austen, but it is not without merit. And there may even be some interesting theoretical notions about life delivered up by the tenured prophets. What is impossible to believe is that enlightenment or correction is the main point of such a bulky book. The New Testament with all the salvational material excised for the sake of moral enlightenment becomes a slim paperback. For better or worse, the New Testament has some other story to tell than moral and spiritual enlightenment.

To describe Biblical religion properly is not easy. The American novelist Walker Percy pointed out the problem when he asserted: "Judaism and Christianity are not members in good standing of the company of the 'world's great religions.' They are not 'spiritual regimes' for enlightenment but they are a life lived." I have already quoted with approval from Franz Rosenzweig on the "belief of a Jew," which is expressed not in creedal statements but in the procreation of the Jewish people. Rosenzweig was obviously contrasting Judaism to Christianity's elaborate creedal pronouncements and dogmatic warfare. But rightly understood, Christianity is also not a creedal *teaching* either. That is the point of Percy's categorization of the two Biblical faiths as outside the realm of the "world's great religions."

The most direct method of understanding the "nonreligious" character of Christianity is to return to "the Founder." As the New Testament states, the problem we face when confronted by the Biblical story is "What think you of Jesus?" Does Jesus conform to the pattern of the great spiritual masters? He does not. The norm for spiritual masterhood is that one be a great teacher of enlightenment, spiritual wisdom, or the tranquil mind. Jesus is not a teacher; he is a savior. The significance of this distinction between spiritual teacher and savior is critical.

Consider a great teacher. Socrates is a good example. Every college teacher claims to practice the Socratic method. Socrates is a master of spiritual enlightenment. In the first place he is "client-centered." He claims to know nothing; he only asks a few little tricky questions. The whole thing is no doubt a bit of a ruse, but the teaching point is profound. Socrates wants to make sure that the pupil is attached to the truth, not to Socrates. It isn't Socrates who wins an argument, it is the truth. Such sentiments are essential principles for *teaching*. A great teacher does not want personal disciples, he wants independent learners who (along with the teacher) stand under the stern judgment of the True—and the Good and the Beautiful if they are currently available. In the realm of "great world religions," Buddha is an exemplar of a great "religious" teacher under the same Socratic self-discipline. He has achieved enlightenment, but that enlightenment is not so much a positive doctrine as it is an ascesis, a method of world-denying that will lead the individual to his or her own enlightenment.

In contrast to these two great teachers, one would have to say that Jesus evidently misunderstands how teaching is played out. Jesus doesn't have students, he has disciples. And not accidentally. Jesus says, "he who believes in *me* shall never die." Not who believes in my teaching, but who believes in *me*. That claim will not get you the E. Harris Harbison Award for teaching. What Jesus "knows" is not enlightenment; he knows the Father. Did he come to report on the Progenitor's state of mind and health? Not exactly. "Only the Son knows the Father. He who knows me knows the Father. Only through me can one come to the Father." Humanistic exegetes are likely to attribute these grandiose claims to the over enthusiastic New Testatment authors, carried away with it all, but it is hard to understand anything about Christianity without taking these statement with some seriousness. If Jesus' only choice was to let us know what he knew about the Father—maybe even as a son knows his father—we might have had a more edifying version of something like *Mommy Dearest* in which Joan Crawford's daughter tells us like it was in the good old Hollywood. Was his mission telling us about Dad? (That sounds decidedly irreverent, but Jesus does refer to the Father as "Abba" which, I am told, is something like "Daddy.") If that had been Jesus' mission he would not then have been "Savior." He would be one in the line of "prophets" who tell us about what the heavens have in mind. Perhaps as the natural or adopted son and heir he might have a special place; like Mohammed he could be the seal of the prophets; last in the line—but a prophet still.

Jesus would still be an interesting figure in the Jewish tradition if he were to be special prophet: perhaps the last or the best. But the sense in which Jesus "knows" the father is not in his reporting on the Divine will and wisdom. One might conclude there had already been more than enough of that in

Isaiah, Jeremiah, Amos, Elijah, and Friends. The traditional Christian Church has always sensed the difference. Jesus doesn't come to give us the Word of God; he claims that he himself *is* the Word of God. It is not what Jesus *teaches* that is the Word of God; it is what Jesus *is* that is the Word of God.

In a salvational religion, one does not reach spiritual 10 by learning about some truth, fact, or person. All that is teacherly and noble, but it is not part of a salvation scenario. In a sin and salvation story, one comes to a new state by living with another. It is entirely possible that my children may one day enlighten me with a piece of spiritual wisdom they have picked up from the Rolling Stones or some other prophetic figures of the modern age. Whether they are ever thoughtful enough to convey such nuggets of illumination my way, my life is significantly changed already because I have lived with them. Yea, verily, I may have come closer to salvation through my kids when they were in diapers than after they have had the benefit of a high school education. Salvational religion depends, then, on "conversion," "resurrection," "radical change" on the basis of a life lived with another.

Any other? Any life with? That is not the New Testament plot line. While it is true that we change a lot with our children, probably it is not enough to be saved. (They would agree.) And the kind of "being-with" has to be something loving, trusting, and sharing. A life might well change from life with another, but like a resentful elder Irish daughter confined to looking after Da while all the others go off to fame, fortune, and America. That life-changing experience is negative and despairing.

To have one's life changed through life with

another is common coin. In the case of the New Testament the relation between disciple and Jesus is proclaimed as "love." The relation is surely not negative—the hatred, disdain, and despair that color whole lives as they disentangle themselves from despotic others. The relation is positive—and more than admiration, respect, emulation. This relation is that affirmation of the other in which the boundary between mine and thine gets hopelessly blurry. Whose life is which? I live in you and you in me. This is an affirmation of the other which does not hold the other at arm's length. If we respect a learned teacher, we respect his learning and his care for his task of teaching. But there is a reserve because he or she has taught us to love learning and the truth, not its ministers and pedagogues. We both stand in self-reserve before the awesome majesty of our high scientific allegiance. Each may sacrifice all for truth, but not for teacher or pupil. But in a salvational relation, there is no ideal which intervenes. It is my life and the other life—it is both lives as though there was one life.

While a great deal of the New Testament may read like a fable, there is no trouble in understanding that for the disciples this Jesus was a figure of salvation. He utterly changed their lives and so they could properly proclaim their "salvation" in and through the life of this one who intervened in their lives. In the words of Yeats's great poem about the execution of the Irish rebels, "Easter 1916": "all changed, changed utterly."

If one forgets for the moment how many baskets of loaves and fishes were collected after the picnic and how many days Lazarus was otherwise detained, the basic story of the New Testament is about a savior in whose life we are supposed to live—and die—and live again. The confrontation here is not one of a *teaching*; the New Testament is not the teachings of Jesus of Nazareth. Buddhism is the teachings of the Enlightened One; Christianity is a relation of our life to this *life* as narrated in the various texts. Jesus "saves" not by pointing a moral way or showing us the truths about life, he lives a certain life which is the salvation of the lives of others. If a Christian claims that in this life of Jesus, he or she finds salvation from sin, it is because in the confrontation with this life one finds a person into whom the whole meaning of human life can be invested.

If Peter and the other fishermen wish to proclaim that in their personal confrontation with this Jesus they met someone worthy of the full expression of their lives, then there is no logical fault in their rushing on to say that he was also Son of God. They would have no other choice. Being the Son of God is not qualifying for a merit badge in magic. If a fisherman were to find a life in which his life could be truly and fully grounded, then he would have to affirm that the other was human but more-than-human. Given our dilemma of freedom, we need some other if life is not to be empty Stoic withdrawal. If we truly believe that this person is the one whom we can *wholly* trust, to whom we always say Yes, then we are somewhat beyond the normal traits available to our rather crabby species. In God we trust, all others pay cash.

Christianity is a salvational religion. It affirms that the meaning for life is expressed in and through a significant other. The meaning of a human life is fulfilled in the love of another which comes upon us as a gift, not in our contemplation or cunning. For the contrariness of human life, the Bible stories tell a singular tale. Whether it is the doctrine of Creation, the honorific treatment of Jesus by the Evangelists, or the notion of Final Judgment, the Bible enjoins against negative life strategies whether in philosophy or philandering. A Creator says that the world is "good . . . very good." In the New Testament, the Powers That Be go beyond a considered judgment and try the creation on for size. Even then, even after shabby treatment, He declares the world wreck is alive and salvageable. Good news is at hand.

There are lots of problems with a declaration of good creation and good news. It just don't seem so! How are we to accept a happy-times scenario when it is so clear that the world is not shaped to human worth. We have not only the testimony of the wise, but consider last quarter's result. Nevertheless, the Bible identifies "sin" as life negation. Sin is depair at it all; sin is prideful withdrawal from or prideful domination of a second-rate world. The Bible says that the right gesture is to affirm just those aspects of the neighborhood that a man or woman of metaphysical good taste ought really to avoid: body, history, and all sorts of disasters even unto death. Small wonder that Biblical religionists have been classified as cosmic masochists. Goodness belongs to the meek and the mauled.

The Bible suggests that no amount of teaching, preaching, and philosophizing is going to persuade a single parishioner that an "affirmative" way of life is "true." When I fall into a teaching mood, I already stand aside from life. I appraise from above and beyond. The more I think about it, the worse the world turns out to be. I turn in my ticket. The affirmation demanded cannot be decided by philosophical judgment because philosophical judgment rests on the fracture of inner worth versus world that the Bible story wants to overcome. He who judges life will find it wanting. The alternative is to live life and form its sense from within. I do not answer the philosopher; I kiss the ground.

Rosenzweig is deeply correct in rejecting a creedal basis for Judaism and locating the "belief" of the Jews in the procreation of the people. The Biblical life attitude is not carried in sage judgment but in the spirit which emerges from an ongoing life. "I cannot give you a judgment on whether the world is good, very good or bad, awful. That is a complicated question. In what sense 'good' or 'bad'? But, pardon me, my children need attending." That is a Biblical conversation.

Living a life, affirming "goodness" in the at-hand furnishings of body and circumstances is not any old live-it-up affair. People who advocate living it up almost always come up with strategies for living (human worth) down. What emerges from living it up is often not a commitment to ongoing life but flight in the face of frustration, inadequacy, and ultimate defeat. The Bible does not say: "Eat, drink, and be merry for tomorrow you die." It does say, "Eat, drink, and marry for life endures."

Rosenzweig's image of procreation is unavoidable. The "solution" to the fracture of worth and our human woe is to live our life in another. We hope to see our worth expressed beyond a narrow self in a worthy object. The salvage of the wreck of humanity is, it is claimed at some length in the Bible, love. It isn't thinking about things that solves the human riddle, it is the insistence of loving. Despite the inexhaustible sentimentality this notion has produced in plaster saints and pulpits exhortations, one can't quite replace it with something hardier.

The problem with "love" as the password for the puzzle is that it falls under the sober judgment of our capacities that we have been pressing all along. Love is one of those big words that live on the right side of human worth. But, like physics and ice hockey, it has to be carried on with inadequate equipment. On the human, all too human level we are not lovers up to our inner worth. Those who preach love as the world's solution often have an extraordinarily exaggerated notion about our abilities in the field.

If love is to be the final watchword, then *salvation* is our life game in two ways. First, if life has value through love, not meditation, we break down self-determination. We bargain away our freehold and accept dependence. Then we become doubly dependent since we rely on the "gift" of the outsider. Whatever else love may be, it cannot be commanded. Love is also poor at calculation. We do not love according to measure. The temptation of love is "beyond measure." If we make *love* the word for life, we are led to deny mere rations and mere "rationality." In so doing, we act in a manifestly imprudent fashion. I trust you too much. I trust myself too much.

Love may be my salvation, but my salvation needs salvation. Loving and being loved on a strictly human level is a prescription for frustration. We need a beloved who can *save* our love. In Rosenzweig's view, it is not that the Jews just go on creating a race. Merely biology might have led to that religious lifestyle. The Jews create the race as the people chosen and commanded by God. It is God's choice of Israel, his free intrusion into their lives, that sustains and perfects their choice for life in loving creation. In the Christian story, it is in Jesus' choice of humanity and our response that we find a life in which we can fully live. One lives in the life of others—the children of the race, the neighbor—in the assurance that our awkward gestures of human love are underwritten, sustained, perfected, and made more sensible by a love larger than even the tribes of Israel could manage.

Christianity is a religion of salvation from sin. It saves us from the natural human negation of the things of this world. It does so through a story of love—living life and its meaning in another. It is by living life in another that sin is overcome. Only in the other can I *live* an affirmation. If I give voice to life I say "yes."

12

Infallibility: An F for Teacher

In the dwindling years of the twentieth century Anno Domini, railways, and religions certainly appear to have seen their best days. Traditional churches in modern Western society have become like the steam locomotive—called on to huff and puff on ceremonial occasions. Given the inherent religiosity of our clan, we can be sure that some vehicle for transcending or getting high will continue: religion is with us for the distance. History is a rich compendium of alternative religious lifestyles, and one can be certain that somewhere between Battery Park and midtown there probably exists a current variant of every single one. Technological transcendence enshrined in Wall Street can meet erotic transcendence empadded in Soho. The IRT carries thousands to inner tranquility far from the madding crowd in the lush verdure of Queens.

It would take the *National Geographic* to sketch in the varieties of theological fauna worship and flora adoring that our ingenious species has constructed.

The array is fascinating for everyone from costume designers to Freudians, but this chapter will concentrate on the traditional church strategies of Western Christianity. Attending to the Church immediately following a chapter on saviors makes good sense not only historically but theologically. Historically the churches came after the events narrated in the New Testament—though there is plenty of suspicion that the "churches" invented the Testament as much as the Testament invented them. Theologically, however, the church is a "natural" next step in our tangled mystery fable.

In the previous chapter we outlined the radical difference between a religion of salvation and a religion of enlightenment. A religion of enlightenment improves our spiritual wisdom or our moral behavior by some teaching. A salvational religion converts our life by leading us to live our lives in another. The notion of a life utterly changed through life with another makes perfectly acceptable sense. To be sure, there may be strong complaints and quibbles about how much or how little one can wring out of normal human encounters. Christians are not pessimistic about human love, though they think it ultimately needs a ground in the giving of self which is the core of the New Testament story. Perhaps one is willing to allow that had one been a tax collector in Palestine circa what we call 30 A.D., one's life might have been utterly changed by meeting this Jesus. The trouble is that Palestine is there, and we are twenty centuries too late.

Alas for theologians, the apostles were literalists. They really believed that salvation was living in the Christ. When the great teacher dies, his teaching may well live on; he may found a school like Plato's academy. He may have a teaching like the Noble Eightfold Path which perpetuates his special wisdom. Even if the teacher leaves no teaching but only the example of an inquisitive mind and the ideal of the Good, like Socrates, the example of the teacher remains to be emulated by later students. All of those means of continuing "the life of the teacher" are eminently sensible and as broadly practiced as the planet is covered with talkers. But that scenario is not the New Testament line. It isn't the teacher's teaching that lives on, it is the "teacher." But if that is how it is, it is no "teacher" but "savior." Since the only way to have a salvational religion is through the intrusion in my life of a strangely significant other, this "other" is indispensable for the ongoing story. Without "resurrection" the story cannot be told. Jesus dies; that is certain biology if not wholly certain history. But if the salvation through Jesus is to be the real thing and not analogized to a story of spiritual enlightenment, then I, lone commuter, must live with this person who so confused the lives of Peter, James, Zebedee, and the crew of the *Galli-lean I*. That doesn't seem to be too easy without aid of H.G. Wells's time machine. How do we *live* with a man who died a rather considerable long time ago (even if he did rise up he disappeared again into heaven with the angels)?

In salvational religion, the savior lives because it is only in meeting this highly significant intervener that the living of my life takes a radical turn. Since this savior is obviously not at a given local address, this "living with" has to be accomplished elsewise. The body of disciples is said to be the "ongoing life" of the savior. Having lived their life in the person of the savior, they die in his death and they live in his rebirth. Their life and the life of the savior are as one. Thus, to live with the savior one may live with the disciples. This ongoing "life" of the savior in the ongoingness of the disciples is what constitutes "the Church."

It is not my intention to defend the *truth* of the church as a continued life of this Jesus of Nazareth. My hope is to demonstrate that this notion of "church" follows in the logic of a salvational religion. The necessity for "church" and its peculiar character is highlighted by the path not taken in this New Testament story. If Christianity were a teaching institution for spiritual enlightenment, all the exotic metaphysics of resurrections, descent of tongues of flames, real presence, mystical body, and other theologico-ecclesiastical apparatus could be happily jettisoned. We all understand that teachers can "live on" in the teachings and that their followers down the decades can continue to propagate their truths and moral maxims. What we don't understand is how the vanished savior can be really present in the ongoing "church." But the logic of *salvation* insists on living with the one who changes my life, not just listening to lectures on elevated topics.

This special notion of "Church" colors the subsequent history of those who claim to be Christians. A notable and highly controversial example of the strange logic of Church is found in the doctrine of papal infallibility. Perhaps no other issue so divides the Christian community as this Roman Catholic claim about the authority of the papal office. The apologists for infallibility defend it as part of the teaching function of the Church. The Pope must speak the truth when proclaiming on matters of faith and morals. In the light of the analysis in this book, however, one could raise a fundamental question about any *teaching* function for this Church. We have argued that Jesus is not a teacher but a savior. The Church is the ongoing life of the savior—perhaps it is no more a teaching body than its Lord is a teacher. If the church is an instrument of salvation and not a teaching organization, what is the point of "infallibility."

What must be "unfailing" for the Church is the continuing life of the savior. If the apostles live their life in Jesus, dying with him and thus sharing in his "resurrection," his ongoing life, then the Church of the twentieth century in Rome, Geneva, or Las Vegas must still be that life. One can be saved only in the life of the salvational other, and the Church is the vehicle for that ongoing life. To have a salvational role the Church must claim an unfailing, single life with that of the initial savior. If the Church is not the continuing life of the savior, then salvation is not at hand.

The unfailingness of the Chruch is the unfailingness of a savior's continuing life. Where does that leave "infallible teaching"? In the most direct sense it is a stranded notion. "Infallible teaching" is a term that has a natural logical space in any respectable teaching enterprise like the world of science. In science there are "teachings" and "teachers," but, unfortunately, we firmly believe that science is as characterized by "fallibility" as Papal pronouncements are by "infallibility." We can *understand* what an infallible teacher might be in science, but we just don't believe that there are (or could be) any. From the standpoint of science, an infallible teacher would be miraculous indeed. Of course, that may be just what the First Vatican Council had in mind when it declared Pius IX to be infallible. (He is supposed to have said that he had always *felt* infallible, but after Vatican I he *knew* he was infallible.) But it is doubtful that miraculous infallibility is either a necessary or a desirable notion. The basic "miracle" of the Church is big enough already—the continuing salvational life of its Lord—not to burden the Christian community with the strange (and unacceptable) notion of infallible teaching.

If "infallible teaching" misdescribes the basic salvation scenario of the Church and is a wild miracle to science, is there anything to be salvaged from the notion? Something. While the Church embodies the ongoing life of the salvational other, this fact is not necessarily a silent fact. There is a delicate balance between what people *do* in life and what they *say* about what they do. It parallels the distinction we have already made between what we do in life and the attitude we take toward what we do. In one sense, the ongoing life of salvation is finding love in the neighbor—assisted by a faith that our shabby gestures are bound into a better whole than we can manage by the Good Samaritan. Thus, the life of Jesus is carried on in the loving gestures of disciples down through the ages. The church is carried in deeds of love, not encyclicals and solemn teachings. From an external point of view, neighborly "charity" may or may not be a part of a salvation story. "Loving" the neighbor may be our sense of shared despair—one warm gesture in a cold universe. There is a special faith and hope to Christian love which is based on certain "beliefs" about the self, the neighbor, and the Universe's interest in the two of us together. Just as it is often extraordinarily difficult to grasp the attitude that lies beneath similar actions, it is also extremely difficult to find the words that formulate the belief or attitude expressed in an action.

The ongoing life of the salvational other is carried at its most immediate level in deeds—loving of neighbor. But this salvational love is bound up with an attitude of faith and hope about the scope and depth of the gestures of love. For Christians, the gesture of loving commitment reaches to the very depths of reality. Love is not cosmically misplaced. It is perfectly legitimate to attempt to state in words the sense of this love. As love in faith and hope, one is inclined to say that this love is based on our participation in the life of another whose love for us perfects our efforts in ways we cannot wholly know or understand—that is the faith. The Church need not be *only* its concentration of loving deeds, it may also try to find words to express the sense in which these deeds are undertaken. Language is not infinitely malleable, and as one fumbles around for a proper way to express the special meaning of this commitment to neighbor, there is an inevitable pressure to start talking about something-more-than-human, God, savior, the ground of my life and so on and so on. The deed-doing disciples find themselves driven to proclaiming that they are acting out the ongoing life of a saving, loving other. Statements congeal; "dogmas" are asserted. This Christian loving is not just any old garden-variety benevolence; Christians insist on a special description of their actions which are signs of faith. They want words to proclaim an unfailing life and love. "Credo in unum Deum . . ."

Are Chruch creeds "infallible"? No, not on their face. What is infallible is the undying Israel, the ongoing ecclesia, the never-failing life of God with us. What we *say* about this fact of ongoing life is the Church's teaching. Church talk, formal "dogma" is derivative. If the talk is a *true* derivative (this is the right characterization in words), then it has a "derived infallibility" but that is all. Because it is extraordinarily difficult to convey even simple experiences in words, one should have a special wariness about the words for death, resurrection, eternal love, and so forth.

The problem with the dogmas to which we are driven is that the words may gradually lose their sense. Instead of communicating the meaning of our actions when we talk about the "hylomorphic union of two natures in one person," we only baffle our interlocutor. Or the dogmas make sense but manifestly fail to fit our deeds. We proclaim salvation and love of neighbor but lead a life of quiet desperation. Worse yet, the Church leads a life of public desperation while continuing to proclaim a message of affirmation and transformational love. If the subtext of this book is correct that neither the New Haven nor the New Testatment is doing very well nowadays, it may well be that this split between proclamation and ongoing life is painfully manifest. Offhand, most people interviewed on the platform at Noroton Heights are unlikely to note church service as one of the livelier, more salvational times of week. Saturday Night Live, but Sunday Morning Deadly is more likely the appraisal.

If churching doesn't seem the liveliest spot in the week, it is quite possible that we don't really know what it is to be alive. The prevalence of sin with all its fun and frolic would suggest that we may not recognize life when it politely introduces itself. If life is essentially frantic, hectic, harried, distracted, and orgasmic, I have attended few church services—even Irish wakes—that were quite like that. But perhaps life is an inner assurance, a center of affirmation, a recollected joy. In that event there may be some hope even for church services.

Love is the proclaimed character of the Christian community. It may well be as immediately absent as liveliness in the Sunday sermon. But in a salvational religion, the love given wholly into the life of the saving other perfects the individual for loving all sorts: even one's neighbors and in-laws. Although the church might well carry on in some theologically subterranean fashion, it is doubtful that it could or would exist over time without the occasional manifestation of the special completeness of love that becomes possible through the moment of salvation. Loving thy neighbor turned out to be a crippled gesture on its own grounds. The grounds of loving neighbor lie elsewhere in a faith that things will go better and nicer than human effort can command. Some professed Christians (and many who never heard of a word of it) live out lives of overcommitted love. The puzzle of these lives continues the puzzle of the original salvation. There is an immediacy to the Christ life in the "saints." Mother Theresa of Calcutta is much and rightly admired, and her life has the marks of overcommitment. There is very little in a human way that can be done for the derelicts of Bombay. She is content to dignify their death. Is her life sensible and practical?

One need not profess any branch of Biblical belief to display the peculiar overcommitment that is the principal message of Genesis, Exodus, on to Acts and Revelation. People have a remarkable ability to misdescribe their actions, and it is the action (and its covert attitude) that is finally determinative. There is, however, a peculiarly religious behavior that separates the professed from the profane but holy. That behavior is prayer. Churching is praying. It is to this peculiar behavior that we now turn.

13

Oh, Fudge!

The time has come to confess to the reader that there is something fundamentally wrong with this presentation. In a strict sense much of what has been asserted in the previous chapters about "god" and allied ideas is either strictly false or strictly nonsense. The falsity and nonsense are inevitable because there is a fatal translation that needs unmasking. It is as if one were to mistake a book on musical criticism for listening to the music. We may attempt to transpose the sense of a sonata into words, but one who only read criticism and never heard music would hardly get the point of the central enterprise. A similar fault occurs here. There is a primary religious performance, and then there is talk about it: theology, church dogmatics, books like this. One might talk about a major chord structure, but without hearing it sounded one would have *no* idea what the reality was like; so we can use the word "god" but unless one repositions this sound into its original composition, the whole discourse floats in empty air.

I imagine that a reader would like to come away from this book able to answer such questions as "Does God exist?," "Who was Jesus of Nazareth—a special friend or relation of His?," "Is Rome right about the *filioque*?" (That would be an interesting reader!) If one is a Christian believer, then some or all of the above statements must be asserted. I am not prepared, however, to say simply that these propositions are true. I will say, however, that these propositions and a long list of others from the traditional catechism are *the right things to say*. Uttering "God exists" in the proper context is good cosmic manners—"the right thing to say."

To illuminate this strange and doubtlessly diffident approach to religious utterances, I want to examine primary religious discourse, i.e., I want to look at the music, not the music criticism. Where do we find primary religious noises? Return to the New Haven or any old commuter line any painful Friday. One of the interesting customs which can be observed as the evening drags through a series of delays is the strange pattern of linguistic behavior. As long as the railroad vehicle is proceeding in some steady fashion, the members of the clan remain silent and composed. However, given some more noticeable breakdown, the silence is broken by low-pitched mumbling sounds which arise spontaneously throughout the vehicle. "My God, now what!" "Again!" "For Chrisesake!" "Damn it anyhow!" "Miscreant whoreson cur!" (a Yale English professor). In addition to such verbalized utterances there will be a number of sighs, suspirations, and ritual gestures: rapid and repeated finger tapping, holding of the head in one hand, in two hands, and so forth.

Mumbling of the type described is characteristic for individuals and groups faced with unfixable frustration. A commuter bothered by sunlight will pull down the shade without incantation. It is only when there is a deep belief that breakdowns are eternal verities that no practical response is made. The commuters utter these phrases and seem to derive considerable satisfaction from the performance—but the utterances are neither intended to describe anything nor to accomplish anything. "Damn it!" trades neither truth or advice.

What is the moral of this muttering? I suggest that "Damn it!" and its linguistic cousins are a fundamental, nontrivial, nonreplaceable part of human spirituality. Cursing is a custom. We all know how to do it and how it works—not at all complicated like writing a sonnet. It is the mainstay of platoon leaders and essential dialogue in films beyond PG. Cursing is a unique, nonreplaceable piece of linguistic activity. "Damn it!" may be uttered *because* I am exasperated, but it is not the same as saying, "I am exasperated." Imagine the sergeant's dialogue which reads not "Scramble your _____, damn it!" but "Scramble your _____, I am exasperated." It won't do. Philosophers have spent a fair bit of time fussing over the logic of statements of fact, contrary-to-fact conditionals, mathematical statements, moral appraisals, and commands. On the whole they have been unable to come up with any place for religious language to fit into this emporium of linguistic turns. My modest suggestion would be that if we look at the logic of cursing we might get somewhere on religion.

As a pioneer on the philosophy of cursing, I am not sure that I will get it all down correctly. I invite other earnest investigators to expand these trail-blazing considerations. *Crescat scientia, vita excolatur*. The first thing to emphasize is that cursing doesn't *describe* anything. Various scatological curse words referring to bodily functions and species of interpersonal relationships are seldom if ever used as referring expressions whilst cursing is in full flight. Aunt Mathilda utters "Oh, fudge!" in perfect exasperation with no intent of referring to the delectable sweet. It would be an interesting experiment and a worthy candidate for the Golden Fleece Award to see if any word or expression could be converted into a curse word by proper intonation. Short Anglo-Saxon words have been favored but that may be mere ethnic parochialism. Perhaps "Intravenous!" has a great future if properly handled. Consider what W.C. Fields was able to do with the unlikely "Godfrey Daniels."

If curses don't add any information to the discourse, they also do not convey any practical command. The sergeant first said "Scramble" and then he threw in the proper epithets. One thing that cursing does accomplish, especially if uttered in a bellowing tone in the presence of suitable witnesses, is that it heightens the emotional atmosphere and gets our attention. The simple act of moving from place A to place B becomes a bustle of fundamental parts in a torrent of malediction.

If cursing was only a raising of the emotional temperature, it might be accomplished by properly modulated screaming. But not every screaming is a cursing. There are screams of laughter and fear which are clearly not in the cursing mode. In fact, compared to mere screaming, cursing has a nice sober quality. This is probably why one may curse to oneself while it is quite impossible to scream to oneself. There is a metaphysical thrust to vintage cursing that needs examination. Cursing is an exasperation phenomenon, and it plays its vital role in human life when the human subject is of the considered opinion that mere practical requests will prove inefficacious.It would be infelicitious to curse one's way through a family lunch. "Pass the salt," will do. In the fatigue and frustration of war, we comprehend the function of "Pass the salt, damn it!" It seems that nothing will cure the endless malaise and trauma of combat, and we permit the transfer of exasperation from life to the simplest request. Not only will there be no peace on earth, there probably won't even be salt on the table.

Vintage cursing, then, occurs in legitimate situations of exasperation. The competent curser knows that a strong oath is unnecessary in life's lesser trials. A rich, round line of blasphemy and abuse is needed when ordinary means have failed. One needs stronger spirits. By calling down God's everlasting malediction on the New York, New Haven and Hartford, Conrail, and the current secretary of transportation—whose name one can never recall—the commuter is summoning powers adequate to the occasion.

Since most accounts of the origins of religion are educated guesswork at best, I would venture my own hypothesis that religion began in efficacious cursing. The advantage of this hypothesis is that it makes our ancient, ancient forebears a little less nitwits than do other hypotheses. Perhaps the favorite account of the origin of religion is that early folk were very bad physicists. Since they couldn't account for lightning by discussing electric potentials, they invented Zeus or some other hot-shot deity as the thunderbolter. But one doubts that primitive tribes were at all interested in even woozy scientific explanation. The immedite response to thunderbolts would be that they are very powerful, highly unpredictable, and likely to scare the bezeus out of you. Thunderbolting has a high emotional valence. Thus, when one talks about thunderbolts one wants to convey the high pitch of the event. Thunderbolts are no sort of thing to be discussed in village street talk. The gods get into the act as a means of hyping the conversation to the emotional level of the experience. God-talk, like cursing, raises the emotional pitch of the event by calling on more-than-human powers as participants in an event.

A piece of evidence for how God-talk gets into polite conversation can be offered from an inscription of Esarhaddon, King of Nineveh, in the seventh century B.C. Esarhaddon is boasting about how he avenged his father, Sennacharib, against his enemies.

> The fear of the great gods, my lords, overthrew them . . . The goddess Ishtar, goddess of battle and fighting, she who loves my priesthood, remained at my side and broke their line. She broke their battle line, and in their assembly they said, "It is our king."

Unlike a modern congressman boasting of his record in office, Esarhaddon palms the victory off on Ishtar. Of course, it is a bit of a boast to have Ishtar on your side, but it would seem to be more glorious to have beaten the Assyrians solo. My guess is that Ishtar gets into the act because Ishtar-talk raises the emotional level of the account to the plane on which it belongs. This victory is no ordinary everyday bargain in the bazaar.

There is more to getting gods on stage, though, than giving the presentation a wide-screen effect. As we noted earlier, some judicious shouting, banging, and horn blowing will raise the emotional temper. There is a deep connection between the master sergeant's ripe blasphemies and Esarhaddon's victory slab. In both instances, a perilous and far from fixable situation threatens. If this battle be won, it will not be with simple human request and command. We need an enspiriting of the troops, and one can invoke Ishtar—a modern sergeant says his troops are full of Ishtar—to accomplish this elevation of the psyche. As physicists, ancient peoples were wretched in conjecturing causes for events; but as group psychologists they were on target when they noted that the proper blend of cursing and blowing of ram horns fit the battle so the walls come tumbling down. The conjecture of the tribal establishment was that in a fix one has to call on more-than-ordinary powers and behaviors to get through. Ordinary old Esarhaddon would have bugged out at the first bugle blast, but full of Ishtar he can accomplish miracles.

Being full of Ishtar leads back to a general characteristic of the cursing tradition. Although it might be possible to convert "Fortran!" into a perfectly well-functioning imprecation and though there is no actual *descriptive* role for good maledictions, there is a natural connection between vintage cursing and a variety of unpreventable bodily functions. The more explosively insistent these functions, the more likely they are to be cherished by the competent curser. Thus, though hunger is an unavoidable fact of life, its onset is so gradual and its satisfaction so regularized that it does not intrude on rational life in the manner of sex or elimination. Few folk have been diverted from life's purpose by a mere rumbling of the stomach, but a stirring of the bowels or a flash in the loins often have the somatic effect of the thunderbolt in a simple drizzle. When the bodily function is used as a vehicle for cursing, it will emerge in its least cultivated manner. It won't do to have the sergeant going around saying "Oh, elimination!" The scientific and polite language suggests that the activity is under rational social control, when it is the *lack* of such control that is necessary in the logic of cursing.

Cursing then is a linguistic activity which raises the spiritual and emotional tone of an occasion by invoking great powers that are felt by the human actors to be wholly or mostly out of their control. Whether the referent is scatological or eschatological, the bodily underworld or the spiritual otherworld, the logic is the same. A mastering power out of the range of human rational request is given the determination of the event. But cursing is not merely a direction of attention to the fact that things are quite out of our control: "Oh Ishtar, what has Conrail wrought now!" Cursing is not redescribing an event in order to get the proper actors identified. Cursing *invokes* the trans-human powers. Esarhaddon was not only a king modestly pointing out that the victory belonged to the Lady, he was also priest who thought that he could invoke Ishtar, summon her to the cause. Thus, no matter how rutty the sergeant's string of curses, the message that is conveyed by the act of verbalization is that these utterly unmasterable, unpredictable, totally powerful forces may somehow be called upon by the human actor. It is not wallowing in the inevitable under-world of bodily function; it is not civilizing them by putting clinical clothes on the raw naked things. It is keeping them at the level of elemental force *and* at the same time saying that just this *elemental* power can be invoked.

The moral of the present lesson is that religious language is rooted in the primitive act of cursing—and its twin, prayer. Cursing and prayer are alike in that they are both forms of discourse which are addressed to powers out of human control; the curse or prayer addresses that power as if it were a something that could be summoned or invoked. In pure cursing, the power is invoked with some de-structive intent; pure prayer invokes for more crea-tive or sustaining ends.

Religion arises both on the ancient desert and in the antique cars of the New Haven because humans do insist on talking when any rational being would shut up. "Damn it!" is an exemplary case. Any sensible assessment of the life situation would di-vide the world into the fixable and the metaphysi-cally kaput. When faced with the kaput dimension of existentiality, the sound thinker will either "grin and bear it" (Stoicism—though they did little grin-ning) or stake out a controllable garden plot (Epi-cureanism). About those things of which one can *do* nothing, one might as well *say* nothing—forget it! Nothing could seem like more prudent admonition, yet a careful statistical survey would indicate that most of us fail that simple test of prudence. Human talk in barracks, bar, and boardroom is obsessed with useless talk. Cursing, ritual lamentations, and poetic fancy are stock-in trade for the breed. Dylan

Thomas puts it well when at the end of a poem on
the inevitable passing of the days of youth he says,

> Oh as I was young and easy in the mercy of his
> means,
> Time held me green and dying
> Though I sang in my chains like the sea.

The image of the human race "singing in its chains
like the sea" will do pefectly for the baseline of what
religion has been all about. Religion is singing—
praying, talking, gesturing—about the humanly
unfixable. That is why religious ceremonies have
clustered about the celebration of our chains—the
places where we are stuck. Being stuck on the New
Haven is like nothing compared to being ontologi-
cally stuck with sex and death. Religions are obsessed with chattering on about sex and its outcomes (the sacraments of marriage and baptism),
and it even insists on having a few last words after
death has finally halted life's incessant jabbering.
Wouldn't you think a decent silence for the dead
would do?

Primary religious behavior is language addressed
at the mute or the mysterious. Language is our
self-conscious communication, and normally we
know how and when it works. We address our
friends and relations and even believe that the dog
understands our tone of voice. Then we find
ourselves talking on when we are not sure that there
is anyone to address yet when we also refuse silence. When we sing our great life songs of celebration and sadness, we can only guess at the life of
the One who slumbers not nor sleeps. We are by no
means sure how to name the Holy Mystery which
we project as the audience for these strange linguis-

tic turns. We guess at the nature of the Audience only from the character of our praying behavior. Theological truths and church dogmas are derivative sketches of how things must be in the light of the persistence of talk. Theology and dogma do not lead to prayer; it is prayer that forces us to try theology and church.

14

And What Does That Prove?

The great Danish theologian Sören Kierkegaard had no use for "proofs for the existence of God." Proofs, he said, were like the traveler who arrived in England and asked a passer-by if yon road was the road to London. On being assured that it was, he proceeded on his journey. Nevertheless he never reached his destination because he had forgotten to ask which direction led to London. So with proofs. They may have some relation to the problem of God, but if traveled in the wrong direction they lead away from the goal, not toward it. I take Kierke-gaard's caution even more strongly. Proofs for the existence of God, the holy, or the "value of religion" will *always* yield the wrong result. Indeed, they lead in the very opposite direction to the one which the prover wishes. Thus, the last thing I would wish for this book would be that it proved anything.

This may seem a disappointing note at chapter 14. All that ink and so little accomplished. But accomplishing a proof for religious matters runs a high risk of dismembering the patient under scrutiny. Suppose that I am asked to *prove* my love. To be sure, I might offer a few comments about the virtues and splendors of the beloved—yet all this would be done with an air of uneasiness. To prove my love is not like proving that the square of the hypotenuse is equal to the sum of the square of the other two sides. I may say "Drat!" if my supposition on this matter is shown false, but basically my self is utterly indifferent to the elegancies of Euclid and his geometry. I am aloof to proof. Not so with proving my love. Indeed, if I were to adopt the aloof-for-proof stance, then I have already subtly yet fundamentally betrayed the love that I have purported to test. Since love is a gesture of my person, since it can be "known" only within the life of my person, stepping outside personal awareness to the distant stance required of proof is to blind-side any positive result. Proving love is like the proof for the existence of God; I undertake it for high ends, but the very act of undertaking destroys the end. My face is already set away from the destination of love as I set out on my road of proof.

This disclaimer of proof is not unusual among believers and theologians. At this point one may sigh meaningfully and say in a low voice; "It is a matter of faith!" To be sure. But the analogy of the lover continues. There are foolish and shallow loves. While love may (should) evade proof, one need not give over to every infatuation and instant enthusiasm. There is something that can be said. This book is an attempt at what to say when proofs are constitutionally out of order. Like the conversation with the instant lover, one asks for a description of the passion, the history of the relation, the biography of the suitor. Obviously something has happened that causes all this suspiration and ardor. Our problem is to fit the words to the passion. What is appropriate to say about this particular state of self and soul?

Theology and the language of church bodies are attempts to fit words to the fundamental utterings: "prayers," of those who have experienced a certain sense of themselves in the world. Faith is a passion before it is words, and the words are rationed to the passion, not the other way around. Yet like all passions, faith can be assayed in talk. This is a grave problem for contemporary religion because some of the traditional words—starting with God—have been so misappropriated that rather than describing and appraising the passion of faith, they end by leading away from London. The sense of the world involved in a radical love is no easy thing to describe. Is it like this? No more beautiful(?), tragic(?), foolish(?). Can I descibe it in a vocabulary fit for humanity—if I even understand that? The claim of this book is that radical love stumbles on toward theological talk—and that properly construed theological talk helps us to understand the strange turns of the human spirit.

Because we are dealing with human beings there is a two-way relation between talk and reality that may not be true for more epistemologically adroit extraterrestrials. For these clever Andromedans or angels, language may be only a dispensable external for their clear and penetrating thoughts. Unhappily for humans, our thinking and our talking get hopelessly tangled. We are more likely to think as we talk than vice versa. We know what we think as we formulate the language in which it is expressed. The great Italian philosopher of art Benedetto Croce used the slogan "No intuition without expression!" Once has every reason to distrust the would-be Beethoven who says that he has these marvelous musicical intuitions but just can't seem to get the right notes onto the paper.

So with life in general. It is hard to imagine religious intuitions without some form of religious talk. Thus, if words like *holy*, *grace*, and *God* are requisitioned to a depository for antique words along with *prithee* and *swounds*, it is unlikely that anyone will have the thoughts that are bound up in those words. Conversely, if these words are mauled and misused, then the sense of "religious experience" to which they point will become hopelessly muddled and opaque. This book is an attempt to express (reexpress) the intuitions that have governed the religious story contained in the basic Biblical story.

If God (the word) and the churches that proclaim that word are in trouble today, it may well be that there is too much concern to "prove" theological claims. The best of proofs leaves the subject demonstrated at a distance. Much church talk also places God at a distance under the illusion that this elevation will demonstrate his importance to the person on the street. The claim of this book, however, has been that any decent divinity is at-hand in the texture of weekdays, not the spectacles of Sundays. The miraculous, the fascinating, and the spooky are entertaining distractions, but they do not speak to the daily anxiety of the human heart. If God is not an interesting oddity but the ground of our life meaning, then He or She must somehow be sensed in the everyday.

External supernaturalism would seem to be the besetting temptation of the more "fundamentalist" religious trends. The Mighty One has done all these mind-boggling feats, and He is also after me to obey the Ten Commandments and contribute regularly in the Sunday collection. If I believed all that, it would be a prudent calculation to adjust my behavior, rather like boarding up the windows before a hurricane. The mightier and more super God becomes, the more I may shrewdly chart a course to curry favor and avoid His wrath—and the less interesting He becomes in my daily rounds.

Sophisticated liberal churches, embarrassed by the supernaturalism of fundamentalist preachers, have their own methods of misappropriating the Biblical texts. If fundamentalists talk too loudly of "Lord Jee-sus!" the liberal pastor may manage to eliminate that subject entirely. Morality is everyday stuff, and so the Bible becomes a set piece of ethical culture. Surely that is not a wicked use of a Good Book, but the busy parishioner may decide that there are more direct methods of seeking ethical instruction that do not involve hymn singing. We decide to read William Safire while contributing to the United Way. Thus is ethical culture enhanced.

Too much (external) God or too little divinity in ethical instruction will lead the rational church consumer to decide to spend the Sunday morning reading the bad news in the *Times* rather than listening to the Good News in the pews. So it goes and so have congregations gone. From the argument of this book, "ethical" religion is not radical enough (it does not reach a God), and fundamentalist religion is radical in the wrong way. It has a god, all right, but he is only a mighty external, a godfather, not Our Father. Both liberal churches and fundamentalists have some sense of the lacks within their traditions. It is not insignificant that Rev. Falwell leads a Moral Majority—up-front divinity could alienate those who share his conservative political interests but not his Biblical literalism. The response of liberal churches is even more interesting. Sensing that there is something only mundane in sheer ethical good sense, some liberal churches have gone for radical causes. "Revolution" is the logical equivalent in liberal churches to miracles in conservative congregations.

Revolutions are in the political order as extraordinary and spectacular as miracles are in the physical order. They are eye-catching spectaculars. If one needs a social gospel with a kick, then some revolution or other is—shall we say—a "godsend"? Fortunately, the modern world, while it lacks miracles of physical healing, is well stocked with revolutionary impulses. Thus, while one may be slightly embarrassed preaching the miracle of the loaves and fishes, a liberal minister may not be at all embarrassed to preach revolution in Guatemala. And there is something deeply correct about this hankering for revoluton displayed by socially alert congregations. The Biblical message calls for a radicalism of love that breaks through the safer barriers of race, class, and nation. The rich and well favored are counseled to love the poor and meek. But the understanding of revolutions—political, sexual, social—in liberal churches may be infected by the same sensationalism that corrodes the theological conservatism of the fundamentalist churches.

The theme of this book since its beginning is that God, if he is to be found at all, must be found at hand.

But the Lord was not in the wind: and after the
wind an earthquake; but the Lord was not in the
earthquake:
And after the earthquake a fire: but the Lord was
not in the fire: and after the fire a still small voice.
(Kings 19:11)

A mighty power who manifests only in earthquakes
and political upheaval would be an awesome superstar, but his or her inability to be a still, small voice
would place this celestial or social show-off in the
category of life experience marked "odd." The story
of God is not a story of the exotic and fascinating—a
story set exclusively in remote occurrences and revolutionary rhetoric. The more divinity is exalted in
miracle and turmoil, the stranger, more distant, and
irrelevant this story is to the average toiler, commuter, and voter—indeed, the more distant this
God becomes to the poor, the oppressed, and the
revolutionary of the earth. Revolution may be the
agonizing battle of breakthrough—but breakthrough to what? Not to more revolution, but back
to the everyday when we may rejoice in daily bread.

The Biblical story suggests a faith in radical love.
We are to trust that our love toward our neighbor
will survive our blundering benevolence and the
other's suspicious acceptance. A realistic appraisal
of the wisdom of our charity is always in order—the
Bible's sinful assessment of the race would suggest
that gushing goodness at neighbors may prove
lethal all the way around. Yet after all possible caution has been added to our warmer impulses we are
encouraged to dare the loving act: to open ourselves

radically to the other, the neighbor, the enemy. This radical openness is a call for revolution, but it is a revolution of the everyday. In a true Biblical analysis, the spectacular revolutions latched on to by avant-garde theologians fail without a mundane radicalism. If God is only in the storming of the barricades, then revolution must be perpetual to be truly blessed. It often seems that radical ministers can hardly wait for the next social or sexual upset to discover the breaking in of revelation. God is indeed in any breaking across barriers to the rejected and despised—but we delude ourselves if we think that category excludes friends, relations, and "our dear self"—to use a phrase from Immanuel Kant. Externalizing the demanded revolution to a distant barrio—important as that undoubtedly is—may ensure that then we come to the aid of the faraway neighbor we arrive filled with self-loathing and a distinct antipathy to almost all our first cousins.

The aim of this book has been to find God in the ordinary—very, very ordinary. Extraordinary deities are impressive but are gods for special occasions, and we need one for the daily commute. The God of fascination was rejected for the God for frustration. Not any old frustration but those checks on our human urges that we cannot solve from the Sears catalog and that are genuine enough to discuss with one's mother, tax adviser, or whoever sorts out the legitimate from the illegitimate desires of the human heart. We concluded that human aspiration is set into some most restrictive bounds. We discovered early on that humans were not the full-fledged deity who was the object of our inquiry. Humanity is set in a stage setting dominated by powers over which we exert only minimal and fitful control. The religious issue became What shall we say about these superpowers? Are they one or many; are they organized or chaotic in their relations to human life? If they are many and disorganized, then our human world will appear in some fashion like the world of ancient polytheism: a realistic scenario of life as lived. But polytheism tends to decay under the human demand for something tidier. We organize the superpowers into some impersonal or personal cartel. We examined one notable organizer, Mother Nature, and found that, though she was awesome, we had a very hard time striking up any conversation. This inability to converse with awesome powers proves to be a determining factor in our spiritual appraisal of the same.

In considering our less-than-divine status vis-à-vis the known and suspected superpowers of the cosmos, we discovered a peculiar aspect of the human species. Short of life and breath as we may be, we are long on essential dignity. The essential freedom of humanity sets us aside and askew with the things of this world and gives us a dignity of appraisal on all things great and super-great. No matter how mighty the Martians or the molecules, humanity assigns the value. Similarly with any proclaimed deity who arrives. It is up to humans, then, to appraise the fix they find themselves in and in themselves. Our appraisal apparatus is much exercised. Humans certainly do expostulate and grump, praise and pray. If the final powers-that-be are mute, we have no mutuality with them and yet—despite good Stoic advice to "shut up"—humans grumble about their lot as if it made some difference.

The fact of freedom casts a fatal spell on the race. Freedom shows that in value and valuing we are more than merely (finitely) human. Give us anything and we will assign it a spiritual price and place. And what place shall we assign to our free selves who seem to hold such sovereign sway in the realm of value? What a puzzle! Infinite in appraisal, finite, all too finite in act. How shall one compose the wild ranges of freedom with the frailities of present flesh?

The Biblical story is one of the spiritual tales humanity tells itself about its fate and fix. What is peculiar about the Biblical tale is that it does not deny the fix. All religious views arise from the collision of desires with limits. What differentiates religious views from ordinary garden-variety frustration is the radical means that religious folk use to solve certain central frustrations. Oriental religions urge us to purge desire so that we may realize that the so-called real world of practical needs and deals in only an illusion. It is false desire that creates frustration. Biblical religion seems to have no great problem with ordinary human desires. Sleeping, eating, and procreating abundantly seem to be part and parcel of the patriarch's vision of the good life. The frustration of the Biblical story lies in our unresolved relation to divinity. Humanity was made in a divine image; humanity in its boundless freedom not only names the beasts of Paradise but values the panoply of creation. How does the sovereign freedom of appraisal fit with the limited capacities of the evaluator? I evaluate my love as "deathless"—but it is not so. In this fix, the temptation is to withdraw in pride or despair; frustration leads to sin. In pride I limit the value to my capacities—as a finite fellow I cut my commitments to my control. I love you according to my fashion, which is to make only rational, returnable commitments. I trust only my (finite) self, which I enshrine as the limit of the world. That is what Christians call sin. Or they call sin despair. I have the urge to overdraw on my emotional reserves, yet I know this leads away from the tranquil mind and the ordered garden. I despair at my fate and curse it or Him. The solution to this divine dilemma of the human species is faith. Faith is not the opposite of knowledge or ignorance; it is the opposite of despair and pride.

The Biblical story for humanity is a story of "god-with-us." The radical dissonance between divine jurisdiction and human action is overcome not from our side but from the other side. There is an at-onement of God and humanity. This at-onement "saves" our commitments unto a better destiny. Should we commit to the limits of our freedom—commit to the point where our life is inextricably tangled with another? Not a safe bet. Neither of us is up to that! But now we are told that the other life is more than the usual finite stuff—it is the life of chosen Israel which we are procreating, it is the life of Messianic Israel, it is the life of Messiah to which we give over our love. Committing to this Messianic other is not commitment to an otherworld, the fascinating, a tourist's temporary wonder. This is "god-with-us." If we *first* commit to this Messianic other, we commit in the same gesture to our at-hand neighbor. "Love the Lord thy God with thy whole heart and thy whole mind and thy whole soul, and thy neighbor as thyself." As we procreate Israel so we live the life of God; or we are emboldened to procreate Israel because it is the life of God. The Christian story does best when it sticks close to the basic Jewish scenario. It is not the procreation of tribal Israel but the continuing life of the Christian community which is procreated. We have the courage of such thorough commitment because the life to which we commit is larger than the local monsignor and the Ladies' Sodality. If God is not with us, it would be best to hedge our bets on both.

The proof of this strange Biblical tale does not come from spectacular wonders. "The heart's a wonder." No stopping of the sun in its revolution or starting of the social revolution will matter much if the tale does not respond to our deepest longing and our deepest worth. What keeps the religious tale alive is too intimate for Cinemascope. Religion is carried in prayer or condemnation as we chug along through the office routine. Religion is the elemental word spoken to the world we experience. We may be silent. Silence answers silence. But if we sing in our chains like the sea, then theology (with a dead or a living God) is the rational deduction from this eternal gabbiness.

The Church is probably in more trouble than our symbolic railway because it has such high-minded defenders. The good old New Haven never was a very pretentious line: a serviceable vehicle for daily commuters. The churches on the other hand have misdigested the radicalism of their message and confused God with the Super Chief. The more that the churches insist on the "highness" and the "specialness" of their theological perspective, the more alien does the whole business become. Karl Barth once criticized liberal, ethically oriented religion by saying that "you can't talk about God by talking about man in a loud voice." I suggest you can't talk about God in a loud voice either. It is a still, small voice.

15

Concluding Scientific Postscript

This book's problem is *tone*. Most immediately it is
the tone of the writing which is likely to be offensive
to piety. Serious topics should not be treated with
sass. I partly agree. Yet the proper tone for the
subject matter is not as simple as piety imagines.
Kierkegaard emphasized "the offense" of Christianity: "a stumbling block to the Jews and a scandal
to the Gentiles." More pointedly, Kierkegaard
thought that the necessity of faith was a scandal
to the wholly scientific outlook of the rational,
bourgeois, practical Copenhagen. It was for this
reason that he entitled one of his major works "Con-
cluding *Un*scientific Postscript." Whatever Christianity was, it was not scientific and, indeed,
appeared like a mere postscript on the solid world of
progressive science that characterized Europe and
fashionable Hegelian philosophy. (For Kierkegaard, an unscientific postscript suggested that the
whole bulk of the latter was radically wrong: P.S.
Don't believe a word of the above. That is a discon-
certing postscript.)

Yet not every offense if properly offensive. There is a proper offense in Biblical religion—an offense, at least, to the modern world's deep belief in its own redemptive powers and its utter rejection of any story of sin and salvation. Amen, but the bantering style of this book may strike Kierkegaardians and corporate CEOs as frolicking on sacred precincts. A philosopher must be a wise man, not a wise guy.

I confess to distinct uneasiness myself about tone. It is much easier to be straightforward and serious on matters which are—in extremis—serious, excruciatingly serious. Death plays a fair part in my meditations, and it is not the normal subject of jibes and japes. I have no difficulty imagining a genuinely concerned religious person being annoyed beyond belief at such "frivolous" philosophizing. I offer a semi-halfhearted-quasi apology. I lack the will to be wholly apologetic. An *Apologia pro Stylo* has both a polemical and a substantive point. Polemically, I would defend my tone at its utmost reaches of offense against much of the prevailing tone of the churches. One can start with the most doubtful: the television pulpits. Lo, what did you turn on the tube to see? A man clothed in soft garments? I confess that when I watch the video pulpits I am always edified by the preacher's hair style. Can that *sleekness* be what this message is all about?

At the other end of the religious performance scale one might put a full-scale *opera seria* at the Vatican Palace. There I am not directly offended. The major actors are so weighted down with robes, ritual, massed choirs, and centuries of expectation and tradition that they are not *personally* pretentious. The liturgical leads disappear into ritual, and one is not confronted with "hard-sell" religion. At best we see a sort of elaborated ongoingness of life. Yet, given some reasons for acceptance, not offense, there remains an aura of showiness, of putting on the dogma, that leaves me if not offended then uneasy.

There have been times when my own suspicious nature about religiosity has been pacified. Reinhold Niebuhr at his height preached with a tension and passion that convinced. I recall an early morning mass at a side chapel in Le Corbusier's church at Ronchamps. But most of my churchly memories seem typified by a conversation with a local pastor. Back in the ancient days when a dialogue mass in Latin was the very edge of radicalism, we had requested that one Sunday service be devoted to this practice. The good monsignor steadfastly rejected the proposal because of the time it would take for all those *"et cum spiritu tuo"s*. As he said, "We wouldn't be able to clear out the parking lot between the masses!"

Religion should be a form of communal prayer, methinks. Great preaching is a form of praying: lifting the mind and heart to God, as the old Baltimore Catechism averred. But being preached at, preached down on? The commercials are preferable. Whisking through eucharist or shabas to clear the parking lot won't do either. Although faith should not be so utterly fastidious that only *that* minister or this "dear little abbey" is the only place that one can worship without offense, there is, I believe, a natural and even properly *religious* reticence toward much of what passes for the public life of religion. If this jokey little book seems out of theological tune, it will at least join much of the rest of the more solemn literature on the subject.

Before abandoning tone, I want to defend this attempt—if not its realization—on substantive grounds. This book's problem is *tone*, not only in the sense of the author's literary conceits, but *tone* is also our subject matter. I do not think that religion aids and abets science (nor does it conflict with it either); morality is basically on its own. If Genesis isn't better Darwin and Moses won't beat out Kant as a moral philosopher, what is religion all about after all after the Fall? This book suggests that it is *tone*. Biblical religion should set a tone for life. Biblical religion discovers no cures for cancer and delivers no moral messages not found in general consumption in other cultures, but it does purport to establish a meaning for science and morality. Where do they fit in the making of my life's meaning? Faith is an *attitude;* it is saying "Yes" when reason might well suggest "No." Yet reason itself is without tone and attitude so that the issue of "Yes" or "No" is wholly in the territory of faith, its lack or loss.

If the argument of the book has come through the surface texture, it should be clear that taking an attitude toward life and the world is not a simple matter of tidying up one's diary and just settling on a life's attitude. It is not clear that we know how to take an attitude toward life. One hardly takes that up like a career in real estate. And even if one sets about it with resolve, the possibilities for self-deception are legion. Would I know my own attitude if I had one? The irresolution about life's appropriate tone is not simple shilly-shally on my part. It comes from the precarious position of the

species which is overburdened with divine pretensions. Vegetables do not strike attitudes. No radish
is a poseur. But human beings, self-reflective subjects as they are, keep striking poses, attitudes, and
tones in a desperate attempt to wear mortality with
style. The conclusion of this book is that mortals can
only dress with grace, with grace.

If setting a tone for life is the fundamental life
problem, it is no less manifest in writing a book on
setting a tone for life. These are the most serious
issues, but one ought not to take oneself too seriously. If, sir, you preach affirmation, pray, sir, why
is thy countenance so gloomy? One ought to wonder at that. Week after week, the Christian churches
preach that salvation has been accomplished in a
tone wholly appropriate for announcing foreclosure
on the mortgage. There are many problems with the
Bible, but its biggest problem is that is has no noticeable sense of humor. Perhaps as God's book it can
set a consistent tone, but for the rest of us some
safety valve may be necessary against self-serving
solemnity or self-humiliating humor. We need the
second-level reflection: I may be hilariously wrong
in trying to be hilariously funny. Perhaps the good
Lord wrote such a serious book so that we would
not take ourselves seriously.

There are great and serious books on religion and
theology. I know because I have stolen all the ideas
in this effort from one or the other of the great
theologians and philosophers. I was moved to write
by an anecdote told of one of the great twentieth-
century churchmen—Dietrich Bonhoeffer. Bonhoeffer's life is surely not a theme for light comedy.
A determined opponent of Nazism, he was impris-
oned toward the end of the war for his complicity in

the plot against Hitler's life and was hanged in the final weeks of the war.

In the 1930s Bonhoeffer came to America to teach for a year at Union Theological Seminary. At the end of this period, he reflected on his experiences. He had not found the theology at Union at the level of sophistication which he knew in Germany. Nevertheless, he quipped that what he had discovered was that "God had not revealed himself solely to German theologians." This could well be the motto of this book. Bonhoeffer's remark is more than clever. Any god worth mentioning surely must have some means of connecting with humanity other than learned discourse. After Kant published his *Critique of Practical Reason*, a correspondent wrote to the aging philosopher and congratulated him on discovering the moral law. Kant was properly horrified. He wrote back saying, in effect, "God forbid that after so many ages of humankind, I should but now *discover* the moral law. What I have done is to give a new *formulation* of the moral law." Morality and religion are too close to their human subjects to wait on the latest issue of *The Philosophical Review*.

If the theologians are not exclusive channels of revelation, the same should be said in a louder tone for the ongoing preaching/teaching life of the established churches. I have already said what I would say about the "infallible life" of the church, but that is a different matter than the conversation that may be drummed up by deacons and archbishops to explain what they are about Sunday in and Sunday out. On that score they are probably worse than theologians. As a matter of fact, I think the theologians have done rather well by the subject matter at hand. What they have not done—and are under no special obligation to do—is convey all this accumulated wisdom in a fashion that is easily accessible to the average literate reader. Mostly this is due to the fact that they are communicating with a specialized audience of other scholars and theologians— though there are moments when I think that they are themselves seduced into thinking that they are saying something more extraordinarily transcendent than the actual interpretation would allow. If this book were merely a kind of prosy translation of that high metaphysical theorizing, it might serve a purpose.

As an example of language which I admire and yet which really won't do for the commuter-believer, I quote a brief summative creed from Karl Rahner's *Foundations of Christian Faith:*

> *Christian Faith:*
> A person really discovers his true self in genuine act of self-realization only if he risks himself radically for another. If he does this, he grasps un-thematically or explicitly what we mean by God as the horizon, the guarantor and the radical depths of this love, the God who in his existentiell and historical self-communication made himself the realm within which such love is possible. This love is meant in both an interpersonal and a social sense, and in the radical unity of these elements it is the ground and the essence of the church.

Rahner, who is a modern Jesuit theologian, suggests that this formulation might be as adequate (and as inadequate) as the traditional Nicene Creed in stating the heart of Christian belief. I believe Rahner's formulation does just that. Alas, it comes at the end of 454 pages of heavy theological trekking. The ordinary reader of *Forbes, Fortune,* or even the *New York Review of Books* will not immediately grasp what *existentiell* means (is it a misprint for *existential?*—which is not very clear either). Words like "unthematic" are more or less ordinary English, but they have a very precise and important meaning in the context of Rahner's developed position. I think that the text of this book says what Rahner says in his creedal formulation. I have attempted to be prosaic with the theologian's metaphors. "Horizon" is a big term for Rahner, and you will find it in this text photographed in Technicolor. "Horizon" is, after all, not a technical term like "megabytes" or "existentiell"; it must have some connection even to the horizon line of the Tetons.

I invite the inquisitive and intrepid reader to take on Rahner for a more serious and scholarly trip over the theological terrain. It will do no harm. When in doubt in constructing parts of this effort, I have not hesitated to translate Rahner into Woody Allen— though it probably comes out like Henny Youngman. Although Rahner has been an immediate source of present aid and comfort, the intellectual debts for the book stretch much further. A philosophical reader will certainly detect a good deal of Kant lurking in the argument. Kant is the philosopher who puts "freedom" at the center of human worth. He also makes good use of Stoicism and the relation between human worth in freedom and the facts about human happiness. Kant finds the discrepancy between free worth and present insufficiency the best argument he can fashion for a *hope* in a Kingdom of Ends and immortal life.

There are two aspects of Kant's argument that I

find uncongenial. In the first place he locates the root of human freedom in reason. Although Kant is one of the subtlest of commentators on that strange human mental power, in the long run I am unsure that "reason" can quite be cleansed from its normal association with theory and abstraction. Which leads to my second demurrer: Kant's system has always seemed to me a machine waiting to be turned on. All the structures are there but what is it like when it actually runs? Kant has the proper structure of the human moral/spiritual life, but what is it like to *live* the life he so dryly sketches out in the *Critiques?* For that answer, I go to two strange characters: Sören Kierkegaard and Jean-Paul Sartre. Kierkegaard is a legend for modern theologians. No one could pretend to do theology in the modern age without submersion in this eccentric Dane who was virtually unknown in his lifetime but whose brilliant literary tales and philosophical analyses invented "existentialism" before the existentialists. The comments on the despair of actuality and the despair of possibility are (I hope) a direct steal from Kierkegaard's great treatise on sin and faith: *Sickness unto Death.*

When I teach philosphy of religion, I usually spend most of the time reading Jean-Paul Sartre. Sartre is the greatest atheist of the Christian tradition. As he himself points out, the Enlightenment rationalists who were more than happy to drop God from their philosophies were not truly atheistic. They believed that they could drop God and substitute the Good so that the whole system of morals and enlightenment remained precisely in place but with a new Holding Company for the basic ethical assets. Sartre takes the nonexistence, absence, death of God very seriously. There is no guarantor for the moral systems of the rational *philosophes*. Or, to put it in terms used in this book: There is no final ground for human freedom. Human beings must invent in a radical way, and they live in a radically absurd situation in which their "transcendent" (the term is Sartre's) freedom finds no final grounding. Lacking a ground for ultimate commitment, Sartre's novels, philosophy, and life (except for Simone de Beauvoir) are records of disintegrating love.

The advantage of Sartre for pedagogical purposes is that one cannot really speak of religion in our society without the other person believing you are engaged in a conversion spiel which will lead straight to the font. Religion has become so manifestly preachy that one searches desperately for a tone for the topic. Since Sartre is a professed atheist, it becomes possible to revive worlds like *god* in a non-collection-box context. And Sartre is a very *conventional* theologian. The God whose absence determines the world is the God of the traditional scholastic theologians and Christian faith. How can God's absence determine the world? Sartre has a superb metaphor describing how an absence determines: I go to the café to meet Pierre. He is not there. I search across the crowd of faces for my friend. But he is not there. The cafe becomes the ground on which the figure of Pierre does not emerge. So, for Sartre, the world is the ground on which the figure of God does not appear for all that we search for him—believing, in fact and spirit, that we had a prearranged appointment.

A final intellectual debt of a less obvious kind is to the modern analytic school of Anglo-Saxon philosophy. I wrote my doctoral dissertation on the grand guru of the school, Ludwig Wittgenstein, and I have learned much from the practitioners of the "school." "School" is the wrong term since it implies a set of doctrines or a fixed method. Neither of those characterizations apply. Analytic philosophy is more a temper of mind: It is in the avoidance of hyperbole, edifying rhetoric, and the sustained metaphor that analytic philosophers maintain a mundane sobriety about their subject. I applaud the sobriety of this turn of mind. Philosophy is difficult enough to do correctly without succumbing to rhetorical self-hypnosis. Thus it seemed to me that a piece of "analytic" work on the grand metaphors of the theologians might prove salutary. Such work is not wholly foreign to analytic philosophers. John Austin, the great Oxford practitioner of ordinary language philosophy, is supposed to have quipped that when God confronted Moses in the Burning Bush and announced himself as "I am," an alert patriarch would have replied, "What are you?" Religion is full of these strangely grand phrases like "I am," but there is much sense is filling in the Austinian punch line.

Most books on theology do run on. Rahner's book gets to a creed on page 454, and this was a summative book at the conclusion of a lifetime of work that produced some three thousand published items. Rahner lived into old age; St. Thomas Aquinas must truly have been an Angelic Doctor since he produced again as much in only thirty-six years. Kierkegaard is no brief essayist, and Sartre is lengthy enough on the other side. The length of the books is not inappropriate. The religious is coextensive with life and the thought of life. Every day could be filled with further reflection. And the